IT'S POSSIBLE

IT'S POSSIBLE

Robert Schuller

Fleming H. Revell Company
Old Tappan, N.J.

All material in this book was originally published
as a syndicated newspaper column.

Library of Congress Cataloging in Publication Data

Schuller, Robert Harold.
　　It's possible.

　　　1.　Success—Anecdotes, Facetiae, Satire, etc.
I.　Title.
BJ1611.2.S29　　　248'.4　　　78-1653
ISBN 0-8007-0927-6

IT'S POSSIBLE

True Hope Redeems the Present

William Cowper is one of my favorite poets. He's been dead for many years, but his hymns are still sung in churches all over the world.

One I particularly like is a song we sang often in our little country church in Iowa. I especially remember the time we gathered together in that church with several other families the day after a terrible tornado leveled our farm. We had lost everything! Every building was gone—literally. We found the remains of our house a half-mile out in one of the pastures. Even our animals, including my horse, were killed.

I can remember singing this song at the beginning of that special service:

> God moves in a mysterious way,
> His wonders to perform;
> He plants His footsteps in the sea,
> And rides upon the storm.

Cowper's songs were not written in a vacuum, for his life was anything but problem free. At one point, he was so desperate that he decided life was no longer worth living. He headed to the river to commit suicide. When he got there, he found the bridge was crowded with people standing around. So he returned home even more dejected.

He decided to try again at home. He went up into the attic, took a piece of rope, tied it to a beam and then around his neck and jumped. The rope broke! Having failed again, he went into his study and took down an old sword that had been hanging on the wall. He held it against his chest and fell on it. But the point hit a rib and broke off. Again, he failed.

Later that evening, he wrote in his diary, "I was suddenly overwhelmed by God's presence and love. I fell on my knees and cried out, 'Oh Lord, be merciful to me, a sinner. Save my immortal soul.' And immediately I felt a surge of new life and hope flow through my being. I was a new person. God's love and mercy were mine!"

From that point on, his life was different. His diary relates problems and difficulties, but there was a new theme of life and hope that overbalanced the struggles. And his hymns reflect his experience of hope in the midst of difficulties.

You can experience that same hope in your life. It is not some empty pie-in-the-sky hope that is reserved for some future day. God offers you hope for today. The change begins when you cry from the depths of your heart, "Oh Lord, be merciful to me, a sinner!"

Break Your Shackles

I have always had a vivid imagination. One of my childhood fantasies was running down the sidewalk as fast as I could, thrusting my arms out and then imagining that I was soaring through the sky, as free as a bird, waving to my friends below.

I believe that on a deep, subliminal level all human beings crave the freedom to imagine, to dream and to soar! The human spirit wants to break free—to be unlimited.

Yet so many people place limits on themselves. Their bylines are "I can't do it," or "It's impossible, it just won't work." They project these limits on difficult tasks, relationships and even on God. And when they project their doubts onto God, that seals their low attainment level permanently.

You can break the shackles of your limitations. By trusting in God and believing that you can have a beautiful life filled with meaning and purpose, you can experience liberation!

Today, you can begin living on top of the mountain, standing under God's heaven and seeing the sunlight and feeling the warmth of His love. Then watch the clouds of doubt and despair slide silently through the sea of space into the outer darkness. The life that is totally yielded to God's power is a life that is unlimited!

Respond Positively

Every problem is a potential opportunity! And you can draw great dividends out of your deepest difficulty if you understand the possibility-thinking perspective on life.

Possibility thinkers see every problem as a project! When you begin to see the problem as a project, the project produces enthusiasm, and enthusiasm produces success. It's all a matter of making the decision to choose to respond positively to whatever happens to you!

You can decide the outcome by your attitude. Remember God never lets anything happen to you unless it is loaded with opportunities!

Face Your Trials With God

"One of the things that I had to learn while in the hospital was how to write and type with a pencil in my mouth," Joni Eareckson explained. A month after graduating from high school, Joni broke her neck in a diving accident, leaving her paralyzed from the shoulder level down.

"I was really upset with being reduced to putting a pencil in my mouth," she added. "But after a while I began to see that it would be a good way to express my ability as an artist."

Holding a pencil tightly between her teeth, Joni began to etch out a drawing. As the picture began to appear, Joni shared with me some of her deepest feelings.

"When I was in the hospital, flat on my back, I was so angry at God. I was not a very pleasant person to be around. But you know, Dr. Schuller, now I can see what God is doing in my life and can see how much closer I've come to knowing Him.

"I don't have the power to face my trials with victory in and of myself," Joni enthused. "That power comes from God. He's the one who sustains me and gives me that greatness!"

Measure of Success

I have a simple definition of success. Success is building self-esteem in yourself and others through sincere service. Success is self-respect. It's that wonderful feeling that comes to you when you have helped others help themselves to a better and more beautiful life.

There is only one alternative to success—failure. And failure is disastrous to a person's self-esteem. Without a successful experience you will remain forever trapped in the impoverished ghetto of a negative self-image. Success turns you around from being a non-self-loving person into a positive person with healthy self-love.

Successful people know that self-esteem is life's highest value. They know the joy of getting is being able to give to those in need. They know the joy of sharing the fruits of success. This great joy is the experience of self-esteem. So building self-esteem in yourself is both the motive and the measure of success!

Start the Day Positively

I begin each day by saying something positive to every person I meet.

I start in the morning by saying "*good* morning" to my wife and to my children, and I mean it! Every morning is good because I'm thankful to be alive!

How do you begin your day? What do you say to the first person you see in the morning? If your first thought is a negative one, do not verbalize it. Hold your tongue until you can think clearly enough to be positive! For you not only set the tone of your day, but the day of others as well.

Say something positive to every person you meet today—begin each new morning believing that life is exciting!

What Is the Price?

I have many fond memories of the years growing up on our farm in Iowa. Those were difficult years financially, and my dad was poor. When he wasn't out working in the fields, he was busy in the small toolshed, where he kept an old forge, a heavy steel-faced anvil and an enormous hammer.

I could be anywhere on our farm, and if he was working with the hammer and the anvil, I could hear the ringing of that hammer echoing from the iron block. I would drop whatever I was doing and run to the shed to watch him at work.

Standing next to the red-hot forge, I would watch him heat the metal until it glowed. Then Dad would place the flaming metal on the anvil and bring the hammer down on it as hard as he could. He would form either an iron frame to hold a pot of blooming geraniums, or perhaps a spare part to repair a plow or some other piece of equipment.

There were other times when I would walk past the old toolshed and hear my father inside. But on these occasions, he was not working with the hammer and the anvil. There were no sounds of metal against metal. Sometimes I would put my ear to the door and hear him talking to someone like a friend. "Lord, I sure got myself a mortgage on this farm. But together we can work it out." Other times he would just talk to God about the kids, or something else close to his heart. These times that he shared with his God were special to him.

And you know, I never knew my father to be lonely. For you will never get lonely as long as there is one person who loves you. And my father believed that God loved him unconditionally. When my dad was together talking with God, he didn't have to play games; he didn't have to wear a mask; he didn't have to pretend he was something he wasn't. For he knew he was loved and accepted.

Do you hunger for that kind of love? Are you willing to pay the price? If you are, you can be confident that God will never condemn you. Neither will He scold you. What is the price, you ask? Simply that you commit yourself to God and open your life to Him and His love.

That is the greatest possibility that exists today. You can be loved and accepted by God Himself. And if you think it all sounds too easy, be a possibility thinker. Go ahead and try. Ask God into your life, and then be prepared for the greatest adventure you could ever imagine!

No Growth Without Pain

"Possibility Thinking is impossible!" a critic exclaimed. "What do you mean?" I protested. "Well, simply this," he continued. "It is impossible to be positive all of the time. To be a perpetual positive possibility thinker is to be a phony and deny the harsh realities of life."

"Oh no," I protested. "The exciting truth is that possibility thinkers have discovered principles which enable them to be cheerful, with sincerity and integrity, regardless of the circumstances!"

We recognize that there is no growth without pain; no progress without separation, difficulties and struggles.

The eagle throws the little ones out of the nest so they can learn to fly. The Bible suggests that we "consider the lilies of the field, how they grow." Lilies grow as their cells begin to swell until they are bloated. Then they burst and separate.

We grow the same way. The child leaves the crib and parents to move out into the world. The mind grows as it struggles with concepts. But the determining factor in the direction of growth is our attitude. My attitude is open and ready for all of God's possibilities—in spite of the circumstances.

A Problem of Theology

The old man returned to the farm where he had grown up as a boy many years before. He wept as he looked upon what was once green farmland but was now acres of black asphalt stained with the drippings of old oil. He gazed at the once noble, gracefully carved hills to see that these beautiful sculptures of nature were now clawed and carved to make room for a nervous assortment of noncoordinated, nonharmonizing structures.

Every place our hands touch, we leave a stain. Some people call it an ecology problem. I call it a problem of theology. For the root of our problem goes deep to a basic imbalance, disturbance and disharmony, not with our environment, but with our creator. We are separated from God.

The cause of all our tensions and all our disequilibrium comes back to a fundamental cause: We are cut off from the source of peace and tranquility. The Good News is that God is waiting to restore that relationship. He's waiting for you. Have you talked to Him today?

A Difference of Perspective

What do you do when you reach the point where the burdens of life become more than you can bear? How can you "get ahold of yourself" when your whole world seems to be falling apart at your feet? Where can you turn when there are no more answers, and you're tempted to blurt out those nasty words "but there's no way!"

There is an answer for those times. A possibility thinker does not deny the existence of problems and burdens. The difference is one of perspective. Instead of focusing on the problems, I focus on the answer—God is able! Faith offers hope. And that hope is based on the power of God.

The Hebrew prophets recognized this. "The joy of the Lord is your strength!" (*See* Nehemiah 8:10.)

The Impossibility Thinker

I confess that I frequently attempt to turn dedicated impossibility thinkers around. One day, while I was waiting for a taxi at the Philadelphia International Airport, I tried to start up a conversation with a gentleman standing next to me.

"Beautiful weather today," I commented.

"Yeah," he said, "but last week was better."

Stunned by his attitude, I tried again. "The sky is so blue, and the clouds are so white," I enthused.

"Yeah," he replied, "but wait until you get downtown. It's smoggy there."

"Well," I thought to myself, "this guy doesn't have anything good to say. But I'll try one more time."

Pointing to a bunch of cars lined up across the street, I said. "Isn't America a great place? Almost everybody can have his own car."

"Yeah," he growled, "but they don't make them like they used to."

Now there is an impossibility thinker! He sees everything from a negative perspective. He turns opportunities into obstacles. He looks at projects and imagines difficulties.

The gentleman was probably right on all counts—from his perspective! His error was in assuming that his perspective was the one and only perspective. He was unable to see what was happening around him through another set of eyes.

No Life Without Goals

I can remember the morning as if it were yesterday. This experience haunts me every time I want to slow down and enjoy the fruits of yesterday's accomplishments.

Up to that morning, everything was going great. In fact, there were no problems at all. As I awoke that morning, I realized I had achieved my objectives. My dreams had come true! And suddenly I felt the pangs of a depression like nothing I had ever experienced before. I had no worries to resolve, no troubles to solve—and I also had no challenges. I felt empty and lost.

Then I had a revelation: One must always have goals beyond today's dreams. There must always be another mountain to conquer. Victor Frankl said it well: "The is must never catch up with the ought!"

The possibility thinker holds in his imagination new objectives, greater goals and loftier dreams. For challenge and achievement are the very ebb and flow of the tide of life. Without them, we are the "living dead." God have pity on the person who catches his or her goals and either will not or cannot imagine greater levels toward which to strive!

See Yourself
As You Want to Be

I was alone in my office early one Saturday when the phone rang. A young lady on the other end of the line asked if I was the Dr. Schuller who had authored *Move Ahead With Possibility Thinking*. I assured her I was.

"Well," she continued, "I want to meet you." Because of my tight schedule, I started to hedge. But she persisted. Finally I asked, "Why do you want to meet me?" When she answered, "I want to see if you are a phony or not," I decided to see her. We set a morning appointment for the next Wednesday.

I had forgotten the incident when my secretary buzzed me and said that the young lady was in the lobby patiently waiting for her appointment with me. I told her to send the visitor up.

Expecting a young, vibrant girl to come bounding into my office to check out whether I was real or not, I was totally unprepared for what I saw. The door opened, and my secretary wheeled a weird contraption into my office. I had never seen anything like it before or since. The woman was wrapped in steel, leather and chains, sitting in a wheelchair.

"Hi, Dr. Schuller!" she enthusiastically exclaimed. I looked closely at all the paraphernalia and found in the center the sparkling face of a beautiful 24-year-old. "I just wanted you to know that after reading your book, I believe in possibility thinking! And I want you to know that if I can believe, then it really works!" she informed me.

I invited Barbara into my office, answered some of her questions, and then listened as she told me her inspiring story. "Doctor Schuller, I am a quadriplegic with cerebral palsy," she began. "Doctors told me that I would never walk or be able to have a normal education. They said that I would be mentally retarded and physically handicapped all my life."

Tears filled her eyes as she shared some of the difficult experiences that she had gone through. "It wasn't until I read your book and started watching your program that I really understood the meaning of the words 'with God all things are possible.' " Barbara enthused.

"I decided that nothing was going to stop me!" she joyfully exclaimed. "That's when I believed that there must be some way that I could have more freedom of movement. I went to doctor after doctor and pleaded with them to help me. But each one said the same thing: 'We can't do anything more for you. You are a permanent cerebral palsy quadriplegic.'

"Finally, after months of searching, I found a doctor who agreed to do as I wished," she explained. "First he put an iron rod between my ankles so my legs couldn't fly out. Then I asked him to design a chest plate with some straps and iron bars to hold my head up. This apparatus would stretch my neck and keep my head from flopping around. And the last thing he did was place a hinged bar between my wrists so my arms could not fly around helplessly. I guess I look like a strange robot from outer space!

"It may look pretty silly, Dr. Schuller," she said, "but let me show you what I can do!"

Suddenly she lifted herself out of the wheelchair and started to walk! She creaked and clanked around my office, her face beaming with joy and pride the entire time. Then she placed herself back into her chair, tired but rejoicing over her incredible feat.

"See, I *can* walk!" she exclaimed.

See yourself as what you want to be! Picture yourself in your mind, expressing the qualities you desire. Lying helpless, Barbara saw herself walking. And against tremendous odds and with great determination, she persisted until she was finally able to walk! Barbara is living proof that what you see is what you'll be!

Exploit Your Assets

Many possibility thinkers I have known are people who had every right to be impossibility thinkers. Like Stanley Stein, who has leprosy. He became totally blind and wanted to die.

One day something amazing happened. This possibility thought came to him: What can I do with what I have left? And it dawned on him that he still had his sanity. He could write a book! And he did!

He went on to write and publish his story in the popular book *Not Alone Anymore*. He summed it up this way: "Instead of bemoaning the things I have lost, I try to make the most of what I have left!" What a way to live!

What's Your Attitude?

In the car on the way home from church, a little boy excitedly told his mother what he had learned in Sunday School. The lesson was about how Moses got the Israelites out of Egypt.

"How did he do it?" the mother asked.

"Very simple," the youngster replied. "Moses hired some bridge experts, and they built a bridge clear across the Red Sea."

"That's hard to believe," the mother laughingly enthused.

"But, Mom," the little boy insisted, "if I told you what they really taught me, you'd never believe me!"

What's your attitude toward the impossibilities you face? Does every solution seem ridiculous? Then you need to develop the attitude that with God all things are possible. The attitude of faith can turn your mountainous problem into a beautiful opportunity!

Stand Tall

I was waiting for my wife and had nothing to do except simply sit and watch the people go by. Some forged their way through the crowd with their eyes glued to the ground.

Others moved briskly with their heads up and their eyes scanning the territory. Nothing escaped their attention.

We walk through life in much the same way. Some are bowed down by pressures and problems, and all they see is the dirt in the roadway. But others stand tall and are the first to spot the light of new opportunities.

When your head is up, you have a different perspective on life. You can see the undeveloped possibilities that lie beyond!

Renew Yourself

I was driving my old car to the office one beautiful morning. As I glanced down at the speedometer, I watched the little numbers change—99,999.8 . . . 99,999.9 . . . and then suddenly it read 00000.0! I had a new car! Brand new, with no mileage on the speedometer!

But when I arrived at my office, I looked at my car. The tires were worn and would need to be replaced soon. The paint was faded and chipped. My car really did not change—it's still the same old sedan.

But the exciting thing is that you can change! Simply invite God into your life by faith and you will "become a brand new person inside. You are not the same any more. A new life has begun!" (*See* 2 Corinthians 5:17.)

Listen to God

"I not only lost my son, I lost my best friend," Mary Pruetzel, mother of the late Freddy Prinze, told me. "I kept asking God, 'Why?' Why my only son?" she added, "but I did not get any answers until I stopped asking and started listening!

"God assured me that Freddy was in a better place and in better hands!" With a renewed spirit, Mary concluded, "Now I don't worry about tomorrow, because it belongs to the Lord!"

God wants to talk to you! He has created within you the spiritual capacity to hear His voice. Find a quiet place. Ask God questions, then give Him an opportunity to answer!

Never Think, "If Only . . ."

Arthur Gordon, a favorite writer of mine, came to New York City to interview Dr. Smiley Blanton, an esteemed psychiatrist. After the initial meeting they both agreed to have lunch together the following day.

As Arthur sat in the restaurant waiting for the doctor, he reflected on his past. When Dr. Blanton finally arrived, he noticed a distant look on Mr. Gordon's face. "What's the matter, Arthur?" he asked.

"Oh, I've just been sitting here thinking about all the 'ifs' in my life," Mr. Gordon replied. "If only I had done this . . . or maybe that."

"Let's drive to my office," Dr. Blanton encouraged, "I want you to hear something."

As he threaded the tape, the psychiatrist said, "I want you to listen to three different people; they are all patients of mine. Listen very carefully."

When the tapes were finished, Dr. Blanton asked Mr. Gordon if he noticed any single trait all the people had in common. He thought for a moment, then answered, "No, I didn't notice anything special."

"Well," the psychiatrist said, "all of them kept repeating one phrase: 'If only . . . if only . . . if only . . . .' "

Those negative words are like a poison. You must learn to replace the negative with the positive! "Next time I will . . . next time, I will!" These positive words point to the future, to a new day and a new beginning!

God can help you as you look to the future. He is picking up the pieces all the time. The prophet Isaiah said, "The Lord will go before you and the Lord will be your rear guard" (*see* Isaiah 52:12). God is not only your rear guard, but He is the vanguard as well. God sees problems coming your way before you do! He will lead you and stand by you!

Trust God to take care of tomorrow. Affirm today that "you will . . . ," not "if only . . . !"

Lock Out Defeat

I remember the story of the old man hired to dig graves in the cemetery by our farm.

Weary from the strenuous work, he sat down and leaned against the inside wall of the grave he had just finished. He quickly fell asleep.

Meanwhile, someone else wandering through the cemetery fell into the same grave. He tried to climb out, but each time slipped back down into the dark hole.

"Help," he anxiously cried, "get me out of here!" His plea awakened the grave digger, who sleepily said, "Who's there?" And suddenly the other fellow got out!

There's always a way out! There is no problem or situation that cannot be solved. Block out the negative thoughts of defeat that lock in your thinking and destroy your motivation. Look for good news!

Choose Success

"My business failed, but it wasn't my fault!"

"What do you mean?" I asked my friend. He went on to describe all the factors that led to his failure—the unions were corrupt, the myriad governmental regulations were backbreaking and the tax structure and competition were lined up against him.

I looked him in the eye and said, "Roy, in the final analysis, you threw in the towel. You gave up. Only *you* had the power to choose failure!" After a moment, he thoughtfully nodded in agreement.

If you fail, you do so because you choose to fail! Failure occurs when we yield to the temptation to take the easier path. Resist that temptation! For there is no satisfaction that can compare with becoming the success that God wants you to be.

Take the Risk

Growing up on the farm in Iowa, I remember many years when Dad needed every bit of corn from last year's crop just to feed the cattle and the livestock. But there was always a corner of our corn bin which held grain that Dad would never use.

"That is next year's seed corn," he would say. "I cannot use it for feed."

Now suppose my father had studied the odds. If he fed that corn to the cattle, there was no risk, for the corn would be productive. But planting that seed in the ground was very risky. Birds could eat it, weeds could choke it, rains could rot it. But—each kernel just might increase a hundredfold. And that possibility led my father to take the risk.

Don't wait because something is risky. Great rewards await those who are willing to take the risk!

Enjoy Faith

"Last year we served over sixty-seven thousand meals in our home, and we didn't spend one cent on food!" Jack Lynd was describing to me how his home for delinquent children operates.

"Our kids help us pray for our food," Jack continued. "And they can really get specific. One time, we hadn't had hamburgers for several weeks, so they started praying for ground beef. A couple of days later I received a call from a man I had never met. He asked if we could use some hamburger meat, and we assured him we could. He sent us one ton of ground meat!"

The secret to Jack's success is his faith. You can enjoy faith today. Trust God! Believe Him! He will honor your faith and turn your impossibilities into exciting new possibilities.

Prayer Is an Anchor

Imagine that you are in a little boat near a sandy beach. You throw out your anchor and pull on the rope until you feel the sandy shore slide underneath. Then you step out onto solid ground.

Now what have you done? Have you pulled the shore to the boat? Of course not, you have moved the boat to the shore.

That's what real prayer is like. Too often we think of praying in order to move God or to get something. The real purpose of praying is to move yourself closer to God—close enough to listen.

God told the prophet Jeremiah, "Call to me and I will answer you" (Jeremiah 33:3 RSV). He'll do the same for you!

Spring of New Possibilities

My secretary handed me the phone message that my good friend Asa had been taken to the hospital.

After extensive tests, the diagnosis indicated a blood clot in the brain. Surgery was imperative. Following the successful removal of the blood clot, doctors informed Asa that he would be confined to a wheelchair for the rest of his life.

One afternoon I stopped by to visit Asa and check on his progress. His wife answered the door and said, "He's out in the backyard. Go on around."

So I opened the gate leading to the backyard and entered unannounced. I stopped short as I saw Asa slumped over in the wheelchair, motionless. But as I approached him quietly from the side I saw that he was looking at the ground through binoculars!

I leaned over the blades of grass which he had been studying so intently. Camouflaged in the ground were hundreds of busy little ants.

"Doctor Schuller," he enthused, "they have really been working hard today!" Then he went on to tell me about the activities of these ants—the homes they had built, and the way they gathered food. He told me about all of the living creatures in his backyard.

"I see love and peace, life and death and resurrection!" he exclaimed. "New flowers are blooming while others are struggling to grow. Sprouts are pushing their way out of the warm soil into the brilliant sunlight. I don't think I have ever been more excited in my life than I am now. I am discovering a whole new world here in my backyard!"

When you go through the valley of trouble in your life, that low spot can become the valley of death, or it can become a spring of new possibilities and new life. In the middle of the darkest experiences of your life, you can still choose to believe that whatever happens to you will prove to be a beautiful blessing.

Healing Force

The setting was the International Psychiatric Convention in Madrid, Spain. I was sitting expectantly in the audience, waiting for the seminar on "Human Values and Psychotherapy" to begin. The first speaker stressed the healing value of faith. "Build faith into the lives of your patients," he exclaimed. "Nothing is more powerful than the power of belief!"

The second speaker was a psychiatrist from West Germany who emphatically said, "Go out, doctors, and build hope into people!"

A Peruvian therapist concluded the program. In his summation he enthused, "Show people love—real non-judgmental love. It is the most powerful healing force in the world."

As I left the assembly hall, I thought to myself, "Wow! The power-packed ingredients of faith, hope and love are the requirements for a positive mental attitude. With these three qualities dominating your emotions you will always be positive."

Ask Questions

Before coming to California, I had never seen an avocado. I went to college and took three years of graduate work, but somehow I missed avocados.

When we arrived in California, all kinds of people gave our family what I thought were some of the biggest, most unusual pears I had ever seen. I tried eating one, but the leatherlike skin tasted horrible. Then I peeled off the black covering and doused it with cream and sugar, but the taste was still awful. Discouraged, I threw the fruit away. Fortunately, someone finally discovered my ignorance and showed me how to enjoy an avocado.

Some of you have thrown prayer away the same way I threw that avocado away. You may have tried to pray, but nothing happened. Or a friend bitterly complained that prayer didn't work, so you gave up. Perhaps you've only been talking to God or pleading with God. Then try two-way prayer. Ask God questions. Relax and listen. Give Him a chance to speak to you. You'll discover how to really pray!

A Better Plan

Several years ago, Linda gave birth to a boy. They were so excited to have a boy in the family that it took them three days to name him!

"Michael David was so beautiful," Linda said. "We finally got to bring him home from the hospital, but after four days, an artery broke in his lung, and we lost him."

Fighting back the tears, Linda said, "He was like an angel that came down to earth for a very short time." God has a special purpose for each life! He loves you and cares about you! Inscribed on Michael's tombstone are these words: HE NEVER LOST HIS WINGS!

Meanwhile the doctor told Linda that she would probably never bear children again—he said it would be a million to one chance. But God had better plans! Linda gave birth to a healthy boy—William Robert!

With God at Center

If a spark of fire falls on green grass, nothing happens. If a spark falls on water or on concrete, nothing happens. But if a spark falls on a powder keg, there's a huge explosion!

When God is at the center of your life, every bad experience that hits you is like a spark falling on water. The power and presence of God dissolve the hurts and resentments, and they simply disappear!

These negative emotions are strangled by God's unending love! They cannot survive!

For "The steadfast love of the Lord never ceases, his mercies never come to an end; they are new every morning; great is thy faithfulness!" (Lamentations 3:22, 23 RSV).

Peace Above All

The story is told that at one time the wisest sages of the world gathered together to discuss the greatest treasures and the highest values.

"The greatest of all human values is fortune," one said. "Money is power!"

Another sage shook his head and said, "No, it is not fortune, it is fame. If you have fame, you can command people. You can change the world."

"No, it is not fortune, or fame, it is family," the third sage exclaimed. "What good is fortune or fame if you are alone?"

Then the wisest of the sages spoke up and said, "Fame, fortune and even family are not enough unless you have peace of mind! Only then can a person enjoy anything else."

"Thou wilt keep him in perfect peace, whose mind is stayed on thee" (Isaiah 26:3).

Faith Defeats Depression

I was walking through the motel lobby when I spotted him across the room. "Ben!" I shouted. "Hello!" He turned around slowly and started walking toward me.

I hadn't seen Ben for years and was thrilled at our chance meeting. He was an avid mountain climber before he fell and broke his back. He miraculously survived, but he still must walk with crutches.

"It's good to see you again," I said. "How are you?"

"Bob," he replied, "I think I'm mentally ill."

"What?" I exclaimed. "Why do you say that?"

Ben opened his heart to me. He had been programming himself negatively. He was depressed with his apparently limited lifestyle.

I told my good friend to never say that he was mentally ill again. "You must affirm," I enthused, "I am mentally healthy and I will continue to be the rest of my life! I will draw my strength from my Heavenly Father!"

We had dinner that same evening and then prayed together before we went our separate ways. In the 24 hours from the time I saw him in the motel lobby to the time he left, Ben was a transformed person.

Affirm the positive—I am free from the power of all negative thoughts! And God's power will flow through you, quickening, strengthening and developing within you joy and beauty!

Stand Tall Today

This morning I was out running before daybreak. What a beautiful experience to run through the silence of the dying night and the about-to-be born morning!

As I was running, I looked up and saw the hills to the east, golden in the sunlight. As I scanned the valley, I saw the still-lingering shadows of the night hugging the earth as if they didn't want to let go.

And that's when I had the revelation! The high hills catch the sunlight first. The sun's rays hit the mountaintops before they reach into the valley. The tall trees are enlightened before the low shrubs. Those who stand tall are the first to catch the glowing rays of the sunlight of a new today!

Stand tall today! And be the first to spot the great opportunities around you!

No Idea Is Perfect

You have wisdom! You have ability! The problem is you don't believe it. You don't believe in your own brilliance or your own ideas. You see something wrong with your ideas, and you really don't think you are as smart as you are. You put yourself down.

Steinbeck told this famous story of *The Pearl*. A man found a beautiful pearl, but it had one tiny flaw. He thought if he could just remove that little imperfection, the pearl would be the biggest and most priceless one in the world. So he peeled off the first layer, thinking it would disappear, but the flaw remained. He continued to take off each layer until finally he had no pearl. The flaw was gone now, but so was the beautiful prize.

No idea is perfect! No solution is without its problems. But if you wait until the conditions are perfect, you'll never get anything done. Get started—today!

You Must Give to Live

In the Holy Land, fresh water comes from a brook and fills the Sea of Galilee. This body of water has always been fruitful in fish. And then the Sea of Galilee takes that water and gives it to the Jordan River. That famous river uses its water to turn the desert into a rose and make it the land of milk and honey.

But the Jordan River ends in another sea to the south which is called the Dead Sea. And, in fact, it is exactly that—a dead sea. It is so salty that if you ever go swimming there, you can't help but float. The reason it is totally dead is that the Dead Sea does not have an outlet. It takes the water in but doesn't give any away! Now that produces the saline problem which makes it salty and dead. Nothing lives in the Dead Sea.

This is a universal principle. If you want to live, you have to give! This is the key to prosperity. Everything we have is a trust from God. Be a good trustee. Be generous. You'll discover a richer life than you ever thought possible.

Don't Play It Safe

What is the spirit of security? It is the deep belief and confidence in yourself. Therefore, insecurity is a lack of faith in one's own ability.

Security, then, is self-confidence!

How can you give a person a sense of security and self-confidence? How can you develop a feeling of security? By taking the risk of building faith in yourself! Self-reliance and self-confidence are the roots of security.

When the Communist system collects people together and shields them from competition, protects them from the possibility of failure and shelters them from the possibility of poverty, is it fostering a sense of security? These may be steps in the attempt to eliminate the fear of poverty and starvation, but the absence of fear is not proof of courage or self-confidence.

Play-it-safe people may eliminate some risks in life, but they also avoid the opportunities to discover self-confidence. They are ignoring the source of security. Security is self-confidence, which is based on God-confidence.

Think Tall, Stand Tall

The person who excels is really an average person, except for the fact that he has a distinctively different attitude toward impossibilities. That's why people who rise to the top oftentimes are not distinguished by their I.Q. or their Ph.D. The difference is their M.A.—Mental Attitude.

Look at the great people in our world today. What makes them different? In almost every case, it is their attitude that makes them willing to tackle a great cause that appears to be impossible. Their attitude gives them the confidence that they can turn impossibilities into possibilities. They think tall, stand tall, and therefore are the first to catch the sunrise of creative ideas!

Fulfill Your Real Inheritance

An inheritance is not a gift—it is a trust! A trust is something that is given to you to take care of and pass on to others.

I met a young man who was getting ready to drop out of school. "My dad is getting rich," he bragged. "He will be dying one of these days, and I will inherit everything he's got."

"Your father is only 41," I said. "He may live to be 90 years of age! Where will you be if he lives to be 90?"

Taken back by my question, he paused and finally said, "Wow, that would make me 67!"

"If you depend upon a family inheritance," I enthused, "you will never be motivated to unlock your own potential—which is the only way to real self-worth and fulfillment!"

As the boy prepared to leave, I added, "If and when you ever receive the family inheritance, remember—that trust really doesn't belong to you—it belongs to the family which came before you and will continue after you. You may use it if you really need it, but otherwise you are to build upon it and pass that trust on to your children so they in turn can pass it on to their children."

You can apply this principle to other areas of life. For example, you are a citizen of the United States of America. You have inherited the freedom to think and talk and work. Many people are living in countries where they do not have the freedom which you have inherited. Assume your responsibility to keep your country alive by protecting it from dangers from without and within. Develop a positive and healthy patriotism, and you will have a greater sense of personal identity and personal worth!

Take My Hand

After years of hard work, Mary Verghese finally graduated from Medical College in her native country of India.

To celebrate, she and several other graduates jumped into a station wagon to go on a picnic. About five miles from the park, the driver attempted to pass a bus and lost control of the car. They rolled over three times before coming to a stop.

Mary regained consciousness five days later, paralyzed from the waist down. Her dream of being an obstetrician was gone! She wept bitterly.

As she lay in the hospital, struggling with God over the tragic turn of events, the words of an old hymn came into her mind: "Take my hands and let them be, consecrated Lord to Thee." Just then one of India's leading surgeons stepped into her room. "Mary," he said, "will you be my assistant in surgery? We will build a ramp, and you can operate from your chair."

Today she is one of the most skillful surgeons in India, working with deformed lepers. Mary asked God for legs— He gave her wings!

Love Lives in You

A good friend of mine claims to be an agnostic. "You really don't know me very well," I said to him as we sat in my office. "Most people don't, you know. By nature I could be one mean, miserable, crabby human being, but I am incurably infected with an unconquerable compulsion to love people—including you!"

My friend stood and walked over to the window, trying to hide the tears. "We all need that beautiful expression of love in our lives!" I continued. And he responded by nodding his head—*yes!*

How can you experience that kind of love? By placing your life in God's hands through faith. For when He lives within you and controls you, love is born. And you will be incurably addicted to loving people!

It's Your Choice

I was walking through an airline terminal the other day and noticed a young lady pushing her way through the crowds. She jarred one man out of her way, and he began to verbally rebuke her for her rudeness. She gave him a quick, cool glance and kept on walking.

At that moment, she was choosing to treat everyone as an object or potential enemy.

Every person you come in contact with has the capacity to become your friend or enemy. But you make the choice by your attitude!

Don't create unnecessary enemies. Create necessary friends. God has given you the freedom of choice, whether it be in choosing friends, a career or a spouse!

Trust in God

A friend of mine who traveled the Atlantic many years ago told me about the time his ship was caught in one of the terrible winter Atlantic storms.

The ship seemed as if it were going to be split at the seams as the storm went on for hours and then days.

"The storm reached a peak one night while all of us were in the dining room," the traveler said. "Mob panic was about to break out! At that point, the captain came in, closed the doorway with his huge frame and began to describe the ship's history: 'This ship has gone through many storms, far worse than this one.'

"Then he began to describe the thickness of the metal plates and the way the beams were tied together. After he finished describing the ship and the storms it had gone through, he said in a strong, confident voice, 'So! We will trust this good ship through!' And everyone felt at peace."

Faith in God has taken many a person through violent storms. Board that ship and believe that God will see you through!

Travel Light

In the play, *Through the Looking Glass*, Alice encounters the White Knight sitting on his white horse, burdened down with an odd assortment of items.

Alice asks, "What are you carrying a beehive for?"

"Well," the White Knight replies, "I may, in my travels, run into a swarm of bees, and if I do, I can catch them."

"What are you doing with the mousetraps?" she questions.

"Well," he answers, "I may just run into some mice, and if I do, I can catch them, you see."

"But what are all those knives around the feet of your horse for?" she queries. "Well, I expect that I may be traveling through some waters, and if I run into sharks, the knives on the feet of the horse will ward the creatures off," he answers.

What a horrible way to travel! The secret of happy living is to learn to travel light. Unload the unnecessary worries that only make for excess baggage. Identify what's really important and eliminate the insignificant, inconsequential items!

Give Yourself
to a Higher Cause

Sadhu Sundar Singh was a well-known missionary in India.

One day he and a friend were traveling up a steep mountain on their way to a monastery. An icy blizzard threatened their lives.

Suddenly they heard a cry for help. Several feet to the side of the path was the form of someone lying half-hidden in the snow.

"We must help," Sadhu exclaimed. "We cannot help," said the other man. "Fate has decreed that he must die. We have no time to spare, or we also will die!"

So the man went on while Sadhu stayed to help his fallen brother. "If I must die, I will die saving someone!" Sadhu exclaimed.

The figure in the snow was a man with a broken leg. Sadhu made a sling out of his blanket and dragged the half-frozen man through the ice and slush.

Then off in the distance he saw a faint light. As they drew closer he saw that it was the monastery. Now he was sure he could make it! But suddenly he stumbled and fell over something hidden beneath the fresh snow. He brushed off the white powder and saw the frozen body of his friend.

In his selfish haste to save his own life, the man lost his life. Sadhu's life was spared because he was willing to risk losing his life helping someone in need!

Be a winner! Lose your life in some great cause today!

Strive to Solve

While visiting in South Korea, I met the head of one of our military command posts. I was so impressed by this man that I asked one of the other men about him.

"I'll give you an example of what kind of leader he is," he answered. "About a year ago we faced an impossible situation. The colonel called in his top engineers and assistants—12 counting myself.

" 'Look,' he said. 'I know we are faced with an impossible situation. So I don't want anybody in this room reminding me! Instead, I want every ounce of mental power spent coming up with solutions! Your job is to dream up a solution!'

"Forty-eight hours later we met again with the solution! He motivated us and the impossibility turned around and became a possibility!"

Get motivated by an impossibility! Great people are average people with a different attitude toward impossible situations!

Never Give Up

Lights flashed on the huge board at the underground headquarters of Fighter Group No. 11 in Uxbridge, Middlesex. Eight men sat around a large wooden table, moving the tiny models of British and opposing German planes which were now engaged in a decisive battle high above their underground fortifications.

Soon the British planes would all have to land and refuel. Churchill told Air Vice-Marshal Park, "We must send up reserve squadrons or the Luftwaffe will destroy our entire air force while they sit like ducks on the ground for refueling. What other reserves have we?"

"None," was the quiet answer.

Then suddenly all the German planes headed eastward! It was unbelievable! Apparently the enemy had chosen the lull in the battle to refuel their own planes. Britain was saved.

Are you facing a personal battle in your life today? God knows how much you can take! Never quit! Never give up, because the tide will turn. A miracle will happen. There is no hopeless situation until you become a hopeless person.

Develop a Plan

If you aim at nothing, you'll hit it everytime! If your goals are vague, your achievements will also be vague. But if your objectives and decisions are specific, you will harvest specific results.

I am amazed at the multitude of people who live their lives according to the whim of the aimless forces of chance. They have surrendered their future! They have abdicated the leadership of their own destiny.

There is still time! You have not failed until you say, "I quit!" Even then, you can begin again. Set specific goals. Develop a plan. And then believe you can succeed. Before you know it, you will discover that people are looking at you and saying, "You're a success! You have arrived! You've won!"

Reaching Goals

Enrico Caruso was told by his first voice teacher, "Your attempt at singing sounds like a raw wind whistling through a window." Caruso refused to listen to her.

Marconi, who invented the wireless, once said to his colleagues, "I think the discoveries of Heinrich Kurtz have laid the way for the possibility of developing wireless communication." The negative thinkers reacted, "That idea violates all known laws of physics!" Marconi refused to listen to them.

Don't listen to negative thinkers! Set a goal for yourself and then persevere as you strive to reach your objective.

"No man, having put his hand to the plough, and looking back, is fit for the kingdom of God" (Luke 9:62).

Believe!

Tommy Lasorda, manager of the L.A. Dodgers, visited with me recently and told of an experience he had while managing a baseball team in the minor leagues.

After losing their seventh straight game, the defeated and exhausted team headed for the humid locker room. When Tommy entered, every one of his players was sitting, dejected, with his head in his hands.

"Hey," Tommy yelled. "Get those heads up! Just because we lose seven straight games doesn't mean we're not a great team. Don't you know the greatest team in the history of baseball—the 1927 Yankees—lost nine straight?"

Suddenly heads went up and expressions changed! The team started to win, and by the end of the season, they were the champions!

I asked Tom, "Did the Yankees really lose nine straight?" "How should I know?" he answered with a chuckle, "I was only a year old then!"

What you believe determines the decisions you make and the way you live. Believe in yourself and you'll be a winner!

Focus on the Dream
for Success

Recently I was asked to sit in on the board meeting of a large corporation. The meeting was with a couple of high-powered realtors, a landowner and an aggressive lawyer. I wasn't in the meeting three minutes before the lawyer became very upset about something. He was so upset that I was shocked at his behavior.

The atmosphere bristled with negative vibrations. I knew that if I stayed around very long I'd be quickly fatigued, and I didn't want to waste my energy. So I said, "When you are able to address yourselves in positive terms and with enthusiasm in a calm and reflective mind, I will be happy to return and rejoin the assembly."

And with that I made a hasty exit.

Later, as I returned to the meeting, the lawyer stormed out. And as soon as he left, the quibbling and the quarreling became even more intense. Finally, I suggested that they all begin to talk about the project that brought them together. As they started discussing the plans, they started dreaming. And as they dreamed, they got excited! As they got excited, they became more enthusiastic! And when they started putting their ideas together, energy came back.

It was fantastic to see the transformation that took place in the room!

Do you need energy? There's plenty available for you. Only be careful which wire you plug into. Power and energy come to you through both the positive and negative wires. But the negative input will produce the energy to worry, become anxious and filled with fear, anger or guilt.

There are a lot of people who use this negative energy to

resist God when He seeks to move into their lives. They are so busy fighting God they end up fatigued and drained.

But there is also a positive wire which produces the power to dream dreams and become involved in projects that create even more energy. These people are open to their God-inspired visions of what could be done, and as they jump into the task, they discover a source of boundless energy that keeps them going. It's that simple!

Great activity is not caused by great energy. Great activity produces great energy!

If you want the energy of God in your life, give your life to God. He'll come in and you'll be in tune with an infinite source of unending, unlimited energy that will recycle itself as you do His happy work.

A Loving Touch

"All I want from my husband is not much more than my dog wants from him," a young wife said in a counseling session.

"When my husband comes home," she continued, "our dog barks and runs to him, waiting for three things to happen: first, a kind look, second, a friendly word—'Hi, Collette!'—and third, a loving touch.

"A look, a word and a touch," she summarized. "That's all I really want from my husband!"

Little effort is required for a kind look and a friendly word. But a loving touch may seem awkward and difficult. Since touching is one of our five natural senses, it is consequently an enormously powerful vehicle of communication.

So allow the positive thoughts to lead naturally to the loving touch!

Add New Insights

I watched my youngest daughter struggle over her spelling one night. I remembered how when I was her age, I would write the words over 10 times. Then if I missed one on the test, the teacher made us write them over 25 times! As I watched her, I thought, "What if I wrote a positive affirmation over 10 times?" And I tried it. It was amazing! By the third time, the words began to take on a new clarity. By the tenth writing, I had added some new insights and the affirmation was mine.

Try it yourself. Think positive thoughts and then write them down until you can quote them word for word. You will be surprised at how fast you can learn them and how helpful they can be!

The Power to Transform

I was so impressed with the young man's smile. His face seemed to radiate a warmth that melted the icy stares of the important executives waiting to meet with him.

Within five minutes the whole atmosphere in the room had changed. The man's friendly personality was infectious, and soon the room was filled with talking and laughter. The meeting was a success.

I cornered the smiling gentleman afterwards and commented on the change that followed his arrival. He shared his secret with me. "Before I enter any room," he related, "I pause and visualize an image of myself as a strong, dominant, friendly, down-to-earth person. I also picture the other people in the meeting as being good friends, returning my smile and reflecting the kindness I want to radiate toward them."

He used his imagination to change people! So can you. Today, firmly hold a mental image of yourself as a relaxed, charming, confident, poised and intelligent person. Your imagination has the power to transform and recreate you and your world!

What God Can Do

"I was on a collision course to self-destruction until God came into my life," Don Newcombe, former major-league baseball star explained to me.

"Then one Sunday morning I was sitting around the breakfast table with my wife and son. We were watching your program, The Hour of Power," Don enthused. "When you asked the TV viewers to join hands and pray with you, I joined hands with Billie and Don, Jr. And after you finished praying, a thrill went through my body from the top of my head to the bottom of my feet. I shall never forget it as long as I draw a breath upon this earth."

His face radiated with joy as he continued, "I felt so good, so clean! I was an alcoholic, but now I travel all over the country representing the National Institute of Alcoholic Abuse. I stand before young people as an example of what God can do!"

Believe the Best

"I've had it with my husband," a young woman shared with me in a counseling session. "He's terrible! I want a divorce," she added with a sense of finality.

I wanted to find out how bad a guy he really was, so I started asking her some questions: "Does he drink too much? Does he gamble? Does he run around with other women? Does he mistreat you or your kids?" To each question, her answer was "No."

"Well, is he a good father to your children?" I persisted. At this, the young lady seemed to calm down and even smile. "Yes, he loves the kids and spends a lot of time with them."

The more questions I asked, the more this lovely wife seemed to appreciate her husband again. Finally, I gently pointed out to her that I was having a very difficult time finding out why her husband was so terrible. She only smiled and thanked me for talking with her.

She had forgotten that love believes the best. Instead of dwelling on the things that bother you about the one you love, believe the best. That's what love is all about.

God Speaks
Your Language

Many years ago, in England, the most famous elephant in the circus world was a huge beast named Bozo. He was a beautiful animal—a great, big, tender hunk of gentleness. Children would come to the circus and extend their chubby, open palms filled with peanuts, through the gate; and Bozo, with tender eyes, would drop his trunk and with a nibbling, mobile nose pick up the treat out of their hands. Then he would curl his trunk and feed himself, almost smiling as he swallowed the gift. Everyone loved Bozo.

But one day something happened that changed his personality almost overnight. He almost stampeded, threatening to crush the man who was cleaning the cage. Then he began to charge at the children. The circus owner knew the elephant was now dangerous and that the problem had to be faced. He came to the conclusion that he would have to exterminate this big old beast. This decision hurt him, not only because he loved the animal, but also because Bozo was the only elephant he had. He had been imported from India, and it would cost him thousands of pounds to replace him.

The owner got an idea. This desperate man decided that he would sell tickets to view the execution of Bozo. At least he would be able to raise part of the money needed to replace him.

The story spread, tickets were sold out, and the place was jammed. On the appointed date, Bozo was in his cage and three men with high-powered rifles rose to take aim at the great beast's head.

Just before the signal was given to shoot, a little, stubby

man with a brown derby hat stepped out of the crowd, walked over to the owner and said, "Sir, this is not necessary. Bozo is not a bad elephant." The owner then said, "But it is so. We must kill him before he kills someone." The little man with the derby hat pleaded, "Sir, give me two minutes alone in his cage, and I'll prove to you that you are wrong. He is not a bad elephant."

The circus owner thought for a moment, wrung his hands and said, "All right. But first you must sign a note absolving me of all responsibility if you get hurt or killed."

The man scribbled on a piece of paper the words, "I absolve you of all guilt," signed his name, folded the paper and handed it to the circus owner, who then opened the door to the cage. The brave man threw his brown derby hat on the ground and stepped into the cage. As soon as he was inside, the door was locked behind him. The elephant raised his trunk, bellowing and trumpeting loudly.

But before the elephant could charge, the man began talking to him, looking him straight in the eye. The people close by could hear the man talking, but they couldn't understand what he was saying. He was speaking in a strange language. The elephant stopped. As he heard these strange words from this man he began to tremble, whine, cry and wave his head back and forth. Now the stranger walked up to Bozo and began to stroke his trunk. The beast tenderly wrapped his trunk around the feet of the man, lifted him up and carried him around his cage and cautiously put him back down at the door. Everyone applauded.

As he walked safely out of the cage, the man said to the keeper, "You see, he is a good elephant. His only problem is that he is an Indian elephant, and he only understands one language. He was homesick for someone who could understand him. I suggest, sir, that you find someone in London who speaks that language and have him come in occasionally and talk to the elephant. If you do, you'll have no problems.''

The man picked up his derby and walked away. The circus owner stood stunned a moment and then looked at the note. He read the signature of the man with the brown derby—Rudyard Kipling.

People also become frustrated, angry and defeated when no one understands them. If you are frustrated and tempted to become angry when you're facing a problem, and you're even tempted to react negatively, check your communication lines with God. He understands. He speaks your language.

God believes in you. God understands your fears, hurts, heartaches and problems. Draw close to Him. He'll show you His plan for you and help you turn your problems into possibilities.

Anger Blocks Creativity

As Leonardo da Vinci was painting the Lord's Supper, one of his aides clumsily spilled some paint at a critical moment. In anger, the famous artist took a brush, threw it on the floor and then spoke horrible words to the young boy. Distraught, the lad ran out of the studio. Alone and deserted, the artist picked up his brush again and reached to paint the face of Jesus. His hand froze. The creativity was gone. Negative emotions blocked any possible creativity. He finally dropped his brush, went out and wandered around the alleys until he found the sobbing young man. He put his arm around him and apologized. "As Christ forgives me, son," he said to the boy, "I forgive you. Come back. We all make mistakes. My mistake of anger was worse than your mistake of spilling the paint." The boy returned with da Vinci. Now, the artist sat down, picked up his brush and creativity returned as he painted the face of Jesus. That face has been an inspiration to millions ever since.

If there is a negative emotion within you, it is blocking you in your relationship with God. "Blessed are the pure in heart, for they shall see God" (Matthew 5:8 RSV).

Look Past Appearances

The elderly man was considered by the townspeople to be both rich and thrifty. His austerity earned him the reputation of a miser. When he died, everyone expected the authorities to find money stashed everywhere in his home. All they found were several gallon cans filled with nickels.

The bank president revealed that the man had used most of his money to help put needy young students through college. And the nickels filled his pockets as he walked down the streets of the business districts looking for cars whose parking meters had expired.

When he found one, he would drop in a nickel. One of his neighbors nodded knowingly and said, "That explains why he looked so happy and contented!"

Happiness is waiting for you right where you are. There are acres of joy under your feet now, along with purpose and enjoyment. All you need to unlock the treasure is a dynamic and positive attitude.

Transform Yourself

Your imagination can transform your physical appearance! Imagine yourself with twinkling eyes, a beaming face and a radiant personality. Then hold that picture in your mind, and you will become that kind of person.

But think of yourself as ugly and unattractive, and your eyes will take on a dullness, your facial muscles will droop and a gloomy appearance will suddenly appear.

Beauty is mind deep not skin deep. For you are as pretty, or as ugly as you think you are. If you visualize yourself as pleasant, friendly, cheerful, laughing and with a sparkling personality, your imagination will turn you into exactly that kind of person.

Begin today to exercise this positive imagination. You will discover that your smile muscles will become so strong that your facial appearance will actually be transformed!

Set Personal Goals

Possibility thinkers are people who believe in setting goals for personal achievement. Almost without exception, these goals initially appear to be unrealistic. But the possibility thinker intuitively knows that with God, nothing is impossible! The motivating force behind this attitude comes from setting goals.

Make up your mind that goal setting is absolutely necessary. If the goal-pursuing human being experiences some times of mental unpleasantness—like worry, tensions, or anxiety—at least he is alive! But human beings without goals to strive for will suffer a far worse fate: boredom. That is a living death!

Not having a goal is more to be feared than not reaching a goal!

Everyday Miracles

Everyday miracles come to us through an off-the-cuff remark or a chance meeting. I was four years old when my uncle came home from China and met me at the gate of our Iowa farmhouse. I was born while he was away, and he said, "So, you're Robert, are you? You ought to be a preacher when you grow up." And he ran into the house to embrace his sister and forgot all about the words he left with me. But I was impressed in that moment. That's when God gave me my calling. That night I added to my prayers the words: ". . . and make me a preacher when I grow up." And that was over forty years ago. The direction of my life was changed by a passing remark.

This week, today, through a chance meeting, God may be trying to say something to you. When God decides to personally move into your life and do something with you, life becomes a series of everyday miracles. Become a miracle spotter.

Don't Quit on Opportunity

I very seldom buy my own clothes. I just don't enjoy shopping, probably because I'd rather be doing something else. So my wife does all my shopping for me.

But one weekend I felt like browsing in one of the quaint little shopping centers in our area. And I thought it would be nice to pick out a new sportscoat. The first shop I entered had sale signs hanging all over the store. "Good, maybe I can find a special buy," I thought.

My eye quickly spotted a beautiful green and white plaid jacket. The colors were subtle enough so that the coat wasn't shocking. I tried it on, and the fit was perfect. I stood in front of the long mirror and admired my good taste. "Hmm, shopping isn't that big a hassle," I thought. I went over to the table with the pants and saw a pair of dark green trousers. They were also on sale! This was my day.

I took the pants into the changing room and put them on. Then I put the jacket back on and went out to see my new outfit. As I was checking it out, the shopowner came over and said, "You know, the green pants don't quite match. And it would be a shame to miss it when you're so close."

"Oh, really?" I replied. "I guess you're right. The colors aren't really the same shadings." So I took the pants off and began to look through the large pile of trousers on the table. There were all kinds and colors, but nothing on sale matched the jacket. As I continued to rummage through the stack, the salesman went over to the rack with the regular-price pants, and chose a pair he thought would match. But as he held them up to the jacket, he shook his head, and said, "They still don't quite match."

We went through every pair of pants in the store. I grabbed a pair of black pants and asked, "How about these? Doesn't black go with everything?"

"Oh, no!" he exclaimed. "Black would look terrible with that coat." I took the jacket off, and he hung it back on the rack with the other coats on sale. I wandered around the store for a while and then finally decided to forego the jacket and look somewhere else. I never did find a coat I liked as much as the green and white plaid one, and later that evening, all I could think about was the shopowner's statement, "It would be a pity to miss it when you are so close." I never did get back to buy that coat. I missed a bargain—and I was so close.

Many people are tempted to quit in life, just as I gave up looking somewhere else for some matching pants. Out of that experience I have many times reminded myself of what that man said to me. When I have been tempted to quit, or give up, I remind myself that "it would be a pity to miss it when I'm so close." And I keep on keeping on.

Some of you have only one more step to take before you enjoy a huge success. Don't stop! Keep on going! How tragic it would be to come to the end of your life and have somebody say, "What a pity that he missed it. He came so close! He quit just as he was about to make it!"

Do you need extra strength to take that next step? I find that the real power behind possibility thinking is the power of God Himself. As I place my faith in His ability, I discover that it is possible! So can you discover that power source. Trust God today!

Overcoming Handicaps

At the age of 18, Frank Vander Maaten was one of the most accomplished violinists in Sioux County, Iowa. Everyone in the area took great pride in his talent and abilities.

One day he was working in his father's blacksmith shop when suddenly, a red-hot iron fell on his left hand, and the four fingers that touched the strings of his violin were severed from his hand! Only his thumb and four short stubs remained on his mutilated hand. His budding career appeared to be finished.

His handicap appeared insurmountable. But not in his thinking! He determined to learn to play the violin left-handed! He held the bow in his mutilated hand and practiced hours every day. And years later he became a prominent violinist in the Sioux City, Iowa, Symphony.

Regardless of your apparent limitations, you are not handicapped until you think you are!

Put Excuses Behind You

I once fell from a ladder and ended up in the hospital for several days. As a result, I got out of the habit of jogging. So when the doctor signed my release, I asked him, "How soon can I start jogging again?" He assured me I could start immediately.

But I found myself making excuses every morning. And all of my possibility-thinking exercises failed to motivate me. I told myself that jogging would increase my strength and that I would be healthier. But still I put off beginning.

One day, an older man asked me why I had quit jogging. As I talked with him, he reminded me of my grandfather, who took long walks every day and lived to be 96. And the more I pictured my grandfather in my mind, the more motivated I became. And the next morning I was back into my jogging routine.

The hardest part of any task is getting started. Don't quit trying. The next thought or next conversation may provide the trigger that sets your motivation level into high gear. And you'll begin to do the thing you know you need to do!

Invent New Solutions

When a high achiever is faced with a new concept and knows that it has never been done successfully before, he is charged with excitement at what he sees as a great opportunity to become a pace-setting pioneer. He is stimulated by the opportunity to discover new solutions to old problems. He is convinced that there must be a way to overcome seemingly insurmountable difficulties. And his creative powers are stimulated to produce amazing results.

Don't wait to start until you see the solutions to every problem. High achievers spot rich opportunities swiftly, make big decisions quickly, then move into action immediately. Low achievers try to solve all the problems first. By the time they are sure they can succeed, the opportunity has passed. Opportunities don't wait for slow moving!

Begin today. You can solve the problems later. When you run into a seemingly unsolvable difficulty, you'll invent a solution!

Be a Pace Setter

One of the most destructive ideas going around the country today is the attitude that yesterday was the day of opportunity.

The truth is there never has been a time in human history that held greater opportunities for more people than our present age. There are vast world problems that we have not even begun to solve, diseases that we have never conquered, and oppressed people that have not yet been set free.

The human race has hardly begun to explore its full potential! You have come along at the best time possible, for we have the tools and equipment.

Be a pioneer and become a pace setter, leaving your fingerprints on the pages of history! The greatest is yet to be!

You Are What You Think

First prize doesn't always go to the brightest or the strongest person. Again and again, the person who wins is the one who is certain of victory!

A young college student scored disappointingly low on his entrance exams and had to use his father's influence to be admitted to the university. But as a result, he developed a terribly low estimate of himself, was convinced he could do no better than average work, and that was exactly what he did. He received just what he expected!

Unfortunately, the admissions test did not really measure this young man's real abilities. Nor did his college courses challenge him to develop the qualities that really determine the difference between excellence and mediocrity—imagination, determination, integrity, sincerity, and intuitive gifts of personal diplomacy.

Later on in life, this man's real talents were developed through his work, and he became one of the most successful men in his profession. He is living proof of the fact that you are what you think you are! Be careful about your opinion of yourself. It will come true!

You Can Unlock Your Future

We have a large, heavy, fireproof box in our home, in which we store important papers. One day, while I was doing some things at home, I needed something out of the box and asked my wife where she kept the key.

"I don't know where that key is," she informed me. "Who used the box last?" "Well," I admitted, "it must have been me, but I can't remember where I put the key." So we began to look through the house.

Finally, after at least an hour of searching, we had exhausted all of the nooks and crannies that could hide a key. "I guess you'll just have to take it to a locksmith," my wife suggested.

So I put the strongbox in the trunk of my car and drove to the nearest locksmith. I was irritated that I would have to pay someone to open the box, but I needed that document. I carried it into the shop and set it down. "I've lost the key," I lamented, "can you help get this thing open?"

"Oh, I think I can find a key for that," the locksmith encouraged me. "Let me take it into the back. You can come with me if you'd like." So we headed to his workshop, and he got a big ring of master keys and started trying each one on the lock. Not one of them worked!

"I'm sorry," he said. "If you'll leave the box, I'm sure the locksmith that owns the shop will know how to get this open. These are complicated locks."

"No," I said, "I need something out of there today. I'll just have to try someone else." And as he went to lift the box to hand it to me, his fingers slipped off the bottom, caught the edge of the lid and the box fell open. My mouth dropped as I looked into the box and saw the key lying on top of the papers—right where I had left it the last time! It had been unlocked all the time I thought it had been locked.

Many of you suffer from that same kind of locked-in thinking. You walk around, all locked up inside yourselves and, as a result, miss the beautiful plan God has for your lives. You think "I could never be as good as she is or as talented as he is." And the future is closed up tight, just like I thought my fireproof box was locked.

But all along, the key is there inside. You can open the door of your future. The key is to affirm the person God wants you to be. Begin to believe in yourself and your possibilities. You can either keep the door closed, by believing it is locked, or you can open the future, by affirming your potential and setting goals that will inspire you and lift your vision beyond your limitations.

God made you and He believes in you. Affirm today everything He wants you to be. You can unlock your future!

What Are You Finding?

Two kinds of birds fly over the California deserts—the hummingbird and the vulture.

All the vulture can see is rotting meat, because that's all he looks for. He thrives on that diet. But the hummingbird ignores the carcasses and the smelly flesh of dead animals. Instead, it looks for the tiny blossoms of the cactus flowers. It buzzes around until it finds the colorful blooms, almost hidden from view by the rocks. Each bird finds what it is looking for!

What are you looking for in life? A better question might be: What are you finding in life? For what you are finding tells you what you are really looking for. Your expectations of life will determine your outcome. Expect miracles and you will find miracles. Expect love and you will find love. Expect joy and you will be filled with happiness.

Sweet Water

A ship sailed from the Orient, heading past South America on a voyage it had never taken before. Unfortunately, it misjudged its water demands, and off the coast of South America the water supply was depleted. The passengers and crew were threatened with sickness and death from lack of water, when a passing ship with a South American flag came by. The distressed vessel signaled "Can you share your water?" The passing vessel responded with "Dip where you are." The distressed captain thought it was an insane command and repeated his request. Again, the signal came back: "Dip where you are."

So a bucket and a rope were lowered, and the captain dipped into the salty ocean, lifted up a bucket of water and put his finger in it, touched his tongue and found that it was sweet. What he did not know was that they were in the center of a mile-wide current in the ocean where the Amazon River was still making its surging inrush into the ocean.

Learn that in whatever state you find yourself, there are diamonds waiting to be mined. Look for the possibilities all around you. God put you where you are, and today you're going to have a wonderful time living, as you practice this faith.

The Power of Hope

Even the smallest possibility thought can overpower many impossibility thoughts, if the possibility thought is given a chance to survive and thrive. One powerful possibility thought, allowed to remain in the brain, has enormous life-changing power.

During the Second World War, England experienced many blackouts. When enemy bombers were sighted, all lights were extinguished. The blackout was total, for even the smallest lighted candle could be seen from miles in the air. You can't measure power by size!

Feed your possibility thought, and you will discover that in an astonishingly short time the mind will be overtaken by the power of hope. It all begins with one small trickle of possibility thinking.

God Is Seeking Us

"If you were Noah and there were a flood today, and you could pick out the people to live with you on the ark to start the world over again, who would you choose?" The question was directed to George Bernard Shaw, the great playwright. His cryptic answer was, "I'd let them all drown!"

I'm glad God doesn't feel that way today! In fact, He is actively seeking each of us in order to fill our lives to overflowing. If you do not have a settled calm at the core of your mind and soul, God's peace is available to you today.

That gnawing restlessness you feel is the result of your soul being homesick for God. Open your life to Him. He loves you and is searching for you this moment. He offers you the gift of peace—peace of mind!

Nothing Can Stop You

God has designed each of us as unique individuals and has given us the equipment and the opportunities to succeed!

This truth was reinforced in my thinking recently as I talked with a young black man who is a member of my church. He told me how, as a boy, he would fall asleep in school because he was so weak from malnutrition. He lived in more than a dozen foster homes. Finally, a foster father said to him, "Just because you're black and poor doesn't mean you can't be successful! You *can* succeed!"

Today, that young man has completed a Ph.D. in psychology at Princeton and is working on his medical degree at the University of California. His turning point came when he started to believe in the words *I can!*

Your life is not a happenstance, nor are you a victim of luck or fate. You are a child of God, and as you give Him your life and become an instrument of His will, nothing can stop you. You can!

The Impossible Dream

The skillful surgeon opened the young girl's skull and slowly lifted her brain out of its cavity. Then he carefully removed the aneurysm and placed her brain back in its place. Her vital signs were good—the delicate surgery looked like it would be a success.

The nurses wheeled Pat into the recovery room where she lay in a deep sleep for four days. On the fifth day, one of the nurses noticed a slight movement in Pat's fingers as she was taking the young patient's pulse. Then suddenly Pat opened her eyes and looked around the room.

Startled by the girl's sudden movement, the nurse took her hand and asked, "How do you feel?"

"Fine," she whispered hoarsely, "but could you please bring me some lipstick?"

"Lipstick?" the nurse laughingly replied, "I guess you're going to be fine."

As the weeks passed, Pat progressed nicely in her physical state, but she suffered from aphasia. Words and sentences became jumbled.

The days became long as she labored patiently to regain her memory and understanding of words. During this time she volunteered to assist in a nursery for retarded children.

One day she was busy working with a five-year-old boy when she noticed a young girl sitting by herself. Pat asked a nurse why this little girl was left alone.

"Oh, that's Janine. She has no possibility for ever developing," the nurse explained. "Doctors say she'll never walk. She's so hopeless, she doesn't even know her own mother!"

"How sad," Pat thought to herself as she walked over to the child and sat next to her on the floor. Janine was tearing paper into small pieces and fluttering her mumbling lips with a finger. It was a pitiful sight. Suddenly the girl stopped her meaningless activity and looked up. Pat smiled and motioned her to come a little closer. Without hesitating, Janine crawled over, buried her head in Pat's lap and began to cry.

Holding the unloved child in her arms, she prayed, "O God, if love alone will do this to a child, what would love plus an education do?" It was at this moment that Pat decided to become a child psychologist.

Before Pat could enroll in college, she faced some obstacles. This determined young lady had to first solve the problem of transportation. She had never learned to drive, and now she lacked the physical coordination to pass a driver's test. So for two years she studied Hawaiian dancing to improve her muscle coordination. Finally she was able to take and pass her driver's test.

Her next stop was to register for some classes, but here she ran into another obstacle. In her first semester, she was placed on academic probation. Her wounded mind could not recall what she had just read, and her grades reflected her problem. Pat read her assignments over and over again in hopes of retaining the material. She underlined chapters and kept note cards so she could memorize the highlights of each lesson. She averaged only three hours of sleep a night during her first year of college! And after all that work Pat managed to pull only a C average. But she wouldn't give up!

Year after year she added up her earned units and finally, 13 years after surgery, she completed her last semester of classroom work, with an average of 4.0! Against seemingly impossible odds she finished her formal studies to earn her Master of Science degree!

God gave Pat an impossible dream. If she had looked at the problems, she would never have achieved her objectives. Pat looked at the victory, not at the battle. She was motivated by the ultimate reward, not by the pain. The secret to her success was her mental attitude toward impossible situations!

What impossible dream has God given you?

True Greatness

The teacher told the class of junior high schoolers to write an essay on "True Greatness." The students could write on the person of their choice who demonstrated this quality of life.

One girl decided to write about her mother. She described how each week her mother would wash a large load of clothes without the aid of an automatic washer or dryer. She would wash each garment by hand and then carefully hang them out on the line to dry.

On the particular day which the young girl described, the clothesline broke just as the mother turned to go back into the house. All the fresh, clean laundry fell to the ground. Without a word, the mother gathered all the damp clothes together and carefully repeated the washing process.

When she finished, she took the clothes and laid them out on a grassy, sunny slope to dry. But just as she completed her task, two large dogs came bounding across the yard, right across the clean clothes.

"My mother did not even get angry!" wrote the young girl. "Instead, she sat down, looked at the mess and said, 'Funny how they didn't miss anything.' I think that's the mark of true greatness," the essay concluded.

The important thing in life is not what happens to us, but our attitude towards every circumstance and event. When we are trusting God and relying upon Him, we can be confident that there are no defeats and no failures.

No Excuse

Being from a large family, I learned the importance of carrying my own weight while still a young boy.

All of us had our chores to do every morning, rain or shine! We had to load hay, milk the cows, feed the chickens and gather the eggs.

I'll never forget those cold, icy mornings when I had to crawl out of bed at dawn and put on my overalls. And if it was raining or snowing, we simply bundled up and went on outside.

One freezing cold morning I ran back into the house crying and complaining about not feeling well. My father greeted me at the door and said, "Just because you have a problem does not give you an excuse!"

I learned very early in life that you cannot make excuses out of problems. Possibility thinkers never turn problems into excuses.

Don't Quit

While jogging early one morning, I thought to myself: *I'll keep running now, but when I'm 65 or 70 years old, I'll be able to quit.*

Then I had a revelation: "As soon as I quit, I start dying. I have to keep running, or I'll lose my physical fitness." So I am going to jog when I'm 70, 80 and 90! In fact, I plan on running when I turn 100! (I'm 50 today.)

Don't ever quit. Don't plan on stopping when you reach the top! Keep on: "But they that wait upon the Lord shall renew their strength; they shall mount up with wings as eagles; they shall run, and not be weary; and they shall walk, and not faint" (Isaiah 40:31).

Details Can Hide the Whole

The art class arrived at the location for the day's painting exercise. They each looked carefully at the scene and then chose a spot to set up their easels and began to record their impressions on the canvas. The instructor had chosen a beautiful pastoral setting.

Throughout the afternoon, each student carefully sketched out the landscape, including the rustic, old barn sitting in the meadow. As the various canvasses began to reflect the colors and textures of the scene, the teacher noticed one of the students working tediously on each individual shingle of the old barn. His canvas was empty, except for the meticulously detailed barn. As the day wore on to evening, this young man continued to labor over his rendition of the shingles.

Finally, the wise instructor suggested, "If you spend so much time painting the shingles you'll miss the colorful glory of the sunset. Don't get caught up in the details to the point where you miss the magnificent whole!"

"The heavens are telling the glory of God; they are a marvelous display of his craftsmanship" (Psalms 19:1 LB).

Wisdom Is With You

There's a story of a man from the Orient who traveled around the world in search of the smartest guru. He was told that the wise old man lived in a cave high up in the Himalayas, so that was his final destination. He loaded his horse down with supplies and set off across the mountains and deserts to find this man of wisdom.

After months of traveling, he came to the foot of the Himalayas. He led his horse up a narrow path until he came to a cave. "Are you the guru who is known for his wisdom around the world?" he called out. He waited and waited until finally the old man walked out into the light, so that he could be seen. "Old man, how can I become brilliant? Where can I find wisdom?" the weary traveler asked. The wise old guru raised his head and gazed into the anxious man's eyes. "Where can you find your horse?" And with that he turned and walked back into the cave.

His horse was with him all the time! Brilliance and the capacity for wisdom were with him all the time. It's right there deep inside you!

Energy Begets New Energy

One morning I awoke when it was still pitch dark outdoors. I had no idea what time it was, so I turned the light on by my bed and saw that it was 5:00 A.M. I was tired but just didn't feel like going back to sleep. So I had a battle with myself on the pillow. "If I want energy," I thought, "the best way to get it is not to spend another sixty minutes in bed but to get out and run!"

Actually, I was too tired to run, which was only proof of the fact that jogging was exactly what I had to do. So I jumped out of bed, got into my sweat suit and started running off into the hills. Everything went fine until in the utter darkness I turned down the wrong road and for the first time got lost while running. When I reached the end of a deadend street, I turned around. A few minutes later I recognized some landmarks.

The sun was just beginning to rise over the distant hills when I found myself home at the front gate exactly 60 minutes after I started my uninterrupted run. I took a warm shower and felt the blood surging through my body! I felt more energetic than ever! I got energy by giving out energy.

Some people are tired because they're afraid they are going to get tired. And because they're afraid they are going to get tired, they don't spend their energy, because they want to save it. And because they are saving it, they are constantly fatigued. If you don't have energy, the best way to get it is to give it out!

Energy is inside of you! But you have to prime the pump! *What you get is what you give! And what you give is what you'll get!* That's a basic principle in life. If you want love from people, you have to give it. And the love you get from people is going to be in proportion to what you give. God is the cosmic source of all spiritual energy! And when you are close to God and in tune with Him you tap the source of energy. "They that wait upon the Lord shall renew their strength" (Isaiah 40:31).

Shields for the Spirit

No discreet person would go into the world half dressed! And no wise person will consider himself well dressed unless his mind is wearing a "positive idea" as a shield against the negative forces that will strike him before his workday begins.

Our family eats breakfast together. Before we scatter our separate ways, we have our "spiritual vitamin" for that day. It is always a Bible verse—short enough to memorize easily, so we can hold it before our minds all day.

You need to dress your mind when you dress your body. Make a hobby of collecting "shields for the spirit" that can fortify your mind. No one is dressed to go out until he has dressed his mind with a fresh, clean, comfortably fitting protective idea!

Give Love

"I remember a dying man pleading with me to trade my cold soup for his little cube of bread," Benno Fischer told me.

Benno, an associate architect of our church, was describing his experience as one of the millions of Jews thrown into concentration camps during World War II.

"I was so hungry and knew that the soup would satisfy my hunger more than the dry bread," he continued. "But this man was dying, so each day I set the tasteless broth by his bedside and slowly bit off pieces of the bland crust of bread.

"When the Americans finally arrived, we were taken to the nearest hospital and given a physical exam," Benno explained. "The doctor told me I lived for only one reason: Out of love for my fellow prisoner, I traded my soup for the bread! The bread had enough nutrition in it to keep me alive. The soup had no source of nourishment."

Loving is giving and giving is loving! And in giving love, you find life!

Give of Yourself Now

I never find it easy to visit a dying person in the hospital. But it is often a very beautiful experience. This past week I stopped to see a member of my church. He is 82 years old and has been a friend for almost 20 years. He knew when they took him to the hospital that he would probably not leave there alive.

As I walked into his room, his lips started to tremble and his eyes filled with tears. "Bob," he softly whispered, "I'm so glad you came."

I took hold of both of his feeble hands as we talked together about heaven and reminisced about the past. As I started to leave, I asked him, "Is there anything I can do for you?"

"Bob," he said, "just keep on being my friend. Keep on loving me!" "I will," I assured him. As I left the hospital, my own heart was full. I felt tremendous ego fulfillment as I gave him love and received love in return.

Give yourself away to someone today. Allow God's love to flow through you to someone around you. You'll discover a sense of satisfaction and fulfillment that nothing can equal. It is the sacrificial self-giving that sanctifies the ego trip.

Aim at Helping Others

Dynamic goals must always rise out of authentic needs. They must always be directed at helping people who are hurting. For that is what keeps you from quitting!

A family in our church owns a business that employs about a thousand people. They said to me one day, "We've made enough money now so that we could retire and live comfortably all our lives."

"Why don't you?" I queried.

"We've thought about it often, but we can't," they continued. "We have all those people whose jobs depend on us. If we quit or sell the business, their jobs would be threatened, and their families might suffer. They just mean too much to us."

My friends are not driven by greed or the push for recognition. They derive a great sense of satisfaction from knowing that their goals and objectives are helping other people meet their own hopes and dreams.

When you aim at helping other people, you're on the road that leads to success!

All Life Is an Echo

The little boy slammed the door and angrily stomped down the path and into the woods behind his home. He headed for his favorite spot in the forest—a calm place where he often sat when he wanted to be alone.

He kicked a couple of branches out of his way and hurled a stone through the trees. In frustration he bellowed out, "I hate you, I hate you!" And then he heard a voice off in the distance repeat what he had yelled, "I hate you, I hate you!"

He looked around to see who it could be and then took off running towards home, afraid that somebody was behind him.

"Mother!" he yelled out as he stormed into the kitchen. "There's someone in the woods! I heard him say, 'I hate you, I hate you!'"

The mother looked down at his little face with his cheeks wet from his tears, leaned down and gently suggested they go and check. When they arrived back at his spot in the midst of the tall trees, she said, "Now I want you to shout as loudly as you can, 'I love you, I love you!'" He let go of her hand and literally screamed out the words, "I love you, I love you!"

All of life is an echo. You receive in return exactly what you give. Give generously of your love, and you'll enjoy a rich harvest of friendships.

God Follows Up for You

I remember the time when my son decided he wanted to plant a garden. Being raised on a farm myself, I knew he was too young, but he was determined!

So we went out to the backyard, found a suitable patch of ground and worked together preparing the soil for the seeds. Later, in the afternoon, the young lad took it upon himself to plant the seeds. He dug a deep trench, poured in some of the tiny seeds, and then covered them over with dirt. They must have been at least a foot underground!

I observed him covering the last of the seeds and rushed outside. "No, Bob," I exclaimed, "make a shallow ditch, cover it lightly with dirt and then pat it down firmly. You planted these too deep!"

He uncovered as many seeds as he could find and tried again. He insisted on "doing it myself." He still didn't do it correctly, but I couldn't tell him much more without spoiling his enthusiasm. Then he ran out to play.

Unknown to him, I went out and carefully replanted the seeds. During the next few weeks, I made sure the ground was watered when he was too busy playing. Then one day the sprouts came up through the soil. Bob was jubilant! "Come quick! Look at the carrots, they're growing! I planted them all by myself!" His face beamed with pride in his successful accomplishment. My labor of love was my secret.

As I reflect back on that experience, I think of the many times in my life when I have done things as awkwardly and as incorrectly as my young son did in planting that garden. But each time in my life, God followed up! He is a loving and faithful father! You can be confident that He is at work in every situation and experience you encounter, actively assisting you for good!

It's What's Inside

A man who was selling balloons on the streets of New York City knew how to attract a crowd before he offered his wares for sale.

First he took a white balloon, filled it up and let it float upward. Next he filled a red balloon and released it. Then he added a yellow one. As the red, yellow and white balloons were floating above his head, the little children gathered around to buy his balloons.

A hesitant little black boy looked up at the balloons and finally asked, "If you filled a black balloon, would it go up too?" The man looked down and said, "Why sure, it's not the color of the balloon, it's what's inside that makes it go up!"

What's inside of you decides whether you succeed or fail, not the color of your skin or your physical construction! Decide to succeed today!

No Gain Without Pain

"When I had painfully regained enough strength to start walking again with crutches, I was so exhausted from the struggle and the torture of physical therapy, I didn't really care if I ever walked again." The young woman who said these words to me had been seriously injured in an automobile accident. After several long, hard months of therapy, she was ready to give up. Then, suddenly, with renewed vigor she started walking again.

"What changed your mind?" I asked. "My therapist," she explained. "He warned me that if I quit, I would lose everything I had gained up to that point. I had to keep on working and improving, or I would have wasted all my efforts to that point."

I've often thought about those words. I believe they express a universal principle of life. We are either retreating backwards and, in the process, dying, or we are growing and moving forward. And there can be no gain without pain.

Escalate Your Goals

As I came down the freeway today, I couldn't help but think back to the day 22 years ago when I drove down that highway for the first time in my life. I was on my way to begin the first service of what was going to be the beginning of a new church.

We were going to meet at a drive-in theater. I planned to stand on the snack bar rooftop and hopefully talk to the people who responded to our ads in the paper and our doorbell-ringing venture.

I picked a peak! It was a church—a nice size congregation with a little building someday. Today our membership exceeds 8,000! When you have a dream and pay the price, whether it's starting a new church, recuperating from an accident, climbing up the ladder professionally or improving personal relationships, you become a better person. You can see farther and you can spot another challenge. The new goal will be a little higher, but if you start small you can make it. You start small, aim tall and then have a ball!

Critical Dreams

"Doctor Schuller, I hope you live to see all of your exciting dreams come true!"

"Oh, I hope not!" I enthused to my well-meaning friend. "Because if I live to see all my dreams come true, I will be dead before I die!"

I begin to die when I stop dreaming! So do you. For our dreams and ideas keep our spirits alive. That's why retirement is a very dangerous time.

When you reach a milestone, or accomplish an objective, that is the critical time for you to set new goals, dream new dreams and discover new possibilities. God has designed you and me in such a way that unless we're committed to something that is beyond our grasp, the process of death and decay will set in. Don't stop at the top!

Rush Into a New Challenge

A group of designers formed a company based on a creative idea they had developed. They struggled with their concept for several months before finally agreeing that the only way they could succeed was to add to their staff a brilliant young scientist from the university in another city. But everyone told them they would never get him to move from his prestigious position.

When it was announced that the man was leaving the university faculty to join this new firm, the news rocked the industry. Asked how they did it, one of the young managers simply said, "We had an idea about something that had never been done before and believed he would be turned on by the possibilities! We didn't get sidetracked by those who said we couldn't do it."

He was right! For a possibility thinker loves to rush into a new challenge. Every unsolved problem is an opportunity. Each opportunity spells adventure. The man or woman who is willing to face the challenges of life knows how to live!

Make Decisions From Strength

"I'll tell you what I am going to do, Dr. Schuller. And you're not going to talk me out of anything!" These words were spoken by a defeated, brokenhearted man whose wife had just deserted him. He was crushed. "What's that?" I asked. And he told me his list:

One, I'm selling my business. Two, I'm moving out of California. Three, I'll never trust another woman. Four, I'll never make any more promises."

"Okay, so you're going to sell your business," I commented. "But what will you do?"

"I don't know," he answered. "That remains to be seen."

"If you're going to move out of California, where will you go?" I asked.

"I don't know yet," my friend replied. "I'm just going to make sure I get away from here."

"And you're never going to make any promises or trust another woman? You know, that means you will never have any committed relationships. Is that what you're saying?" I asked.

"You better believe it," he doggedly affirmed.

I stopped talking to him and started talking to God. I was faced with a man who desperately needed help. And all of the education in the world doesn't provide any answers to some of the questions asked by grieving people. "Help me, Lord," I prayed, "to advise this bitter man as you would."

I'll never forget the answer that God gave me for him. I looked at this hurt and angry man and said, "You are making one big mistake." Puzzled, he looked up at me and asked, "What's that?" I continued: "You are making permanent, irreversible negative decisions when you are at your worst, not when you are at your best. Right now, you are not in the best frame of mind. In fact, you are probably weaker than you have ever been. You must never forget this—never make negative decisions in dark times. Ride out the storm! Don't make any rash, irreversible, negative decisions when you are distressed. You can't trust your judgment when you are down.''

"What do you mean?" he asked.

"It's quite simple," I explained. "You say your business has been doing well. Suppose two years from now things cool off, and you wish you had your business back again. Can you pick it up just like that?''

"I guess not," he said.

"Suppose in a year or two you meet some beautiful woman, and the two of you have the capacity to love and to trust each other. If you make a decision today that you're never going to give another person a chance to love and be loved by you, you'll deprive yourself of great joy.''

One of the greatest tragedies of life is to make future plans in times of personal despair. These people are in the valley. They are hatching ideas out of reactionary moments of personal defeat or setbacks. So these failure-prone people are trapped in an emotionally deprived ghetto of underachievement, failure and poverty. They are making decisions out of weakness rather than out of strength.

What do you do when you are in the slough, or in the valley, or in the bottom of the canyon? You sit tight, keep hoping, pray deeply and continue to struggle! When you're strong and thinking at your best, that's the time for action! When you are down in the slough, do not believe in the shadows, or you will become entrapped as a child of darkness.

"While there is light, believe in the light, that you might become children of light!" (*See* John 12:36.)

Faith Can Make You Strong

Several hands went up in the air as curious students volunteered for an experiment using hypnosis.

The professor chose a young man who seemed especially eager and asked him to come to the front of the class. The whole room became silent as each person anticipated something unusual.

"I want you to take this dynamometer and exert as much pressure as you possibly can," the instructor explained. The volunteer took a firm grip and pressed as hard as he could, until the meter registered 101 pounds of pressure.

Then the young man was instructed to sit down in a comfortable chair. "I am going to hypnotize you and then ask you to repeat what you have just done," he was told. Under hypnosis, the student was told to exert pressure on the instrument, but that his strength was gone. He was told that he would be very weak. And this time the scale measured only 29 pounds of pressure.

Then the teacher suggested to the volunteer, who was still hypnotized, that his strength had returned and that now he was even stronger than before. "Go ahead and try again," he was encouraged. And this time the scale registered 142 pounds of pressure.

We hypnotize ourselves all the time. When we think we can't, we won't. And if we affirm those positive words, "I can," we discover we can. "As a man thinks in his heart, so is he!" (*See* Proverbs 23:7.)

Use Self-Confidence

Leaning back in his large, executive chair, the newly promoted colonel propped his feet up on his beautiful new desk. As he glanced around his new, enlarged office and then at the "birds" on his shoulders, he had to admit it felt good.

As he sat there basking in his newly found glory, an airman stepped in and saluted. "Sir, . . ." but before he could continue, the colonel interrupted him and said, "Just a minute, young man, I have to take a call. My secretary just buzzed me before you stepped in."

He reached over and picked up the phone and said, "Hello. Oh, hello, General. Yes, yes, I'll telephone the President immediately." As he put down the receiver, he smiled at the young man standing there and then boastfully asked, "Now, what can I do for you?"

"Oh, nothing, Colonel," he hesitantly replied. "I was sent here to connect your phone, but it looks like you've already done it . . . sir."

Insecure people get themselves into all kinds of hot water! Develop a self-confident, self-affirming, self-reliant, positive self-image. Get it, use it and keep working on it. For the picture you have of yourself is the person you most certainly will become!

Never Retire From Life

It was an exciting evening! An atmosphere of celebration filled the auditorium where over one hundred graduates were to receive their bachelor's degrees from Pepperdine University. I was there to receive an honorary degree and to deliver the commencement address. After I finished my speech I returned to my seat to watch the awarding of the degrees.

The impressive ceremony was moving along smoothly when suddenly there was a loud cheer and several children started shouting, "You did it, Grandma! You finally made it!" The whole auditorium broke into spontaneous applause as a gray-haired woman came striding across the platform to accept her diploma.

Afterwards, I had the opportunity to talk with her and meet most of her 10 children and 27 grandchildren. She was a young, vibrant woman of 67 who was not content with the idea of retirement. So she set new goals for herself and was very proud of having realized one of her lifetime dreams—graduating from college.

I don't ever plan to retire, either. I plan on staying young and enthused by continuing to set new goals and dreaming of brighter objectives. That's a guaranteed way to stay alive and young all your life!

Dreams Survive in Hope

My daughter Sheila was flying back East to enroll in college. When she left, it marked the beginning of a new phase in our family. I drove her to the airport, and we rode silently down the freeway.

Finally I said, "Sheila, what are you thinking?" "Oh, I was just remembering, Dad, some words you said in one of your sermons." "Oh?" I replied, "that's interesting. What were they?"

She turned, looked at me, and with a smile on her face and tears in her eyes, she quoted these words: "Grieve not for me, who is about to start a new adventure. Eager I stand, and ready to depart, me and my reckless pioneering heart."

Words filled with hope! My own eyes became misty as we talked together about her hopes and dreams for the future. Hope must be at the beginning, in the middle and at the end. Without hope, dreams fade, decisions go unmade and opportunities pass by. But when you have hope, your dreams take root. And where there is hope, there is life!

The Choice Is Yours

I suspect that at the end of my life someone will say, "Schuller? He was a big failure . . . in golf!" And that evaluation would be very accurate. I am a failure at golf. I used to play, but my scores were so terrible I gave up and quit.

Someone else could say that I am a failure at tennis. And they would be correct. But the important principle behind my failure is that I have chosen to be a failure in these sports. At one point, I purposely decided to divert my time and energies away from these activities so that I could invest myself in other areas. I chose to fail in golf and tennis so that I could succeed in something else!

You will succeed or fail based on the decisions you make! You fail because you choose to fail. Failure cannot be blamed on anyone or anything else. Only you have the power to make that decision. Only you can choose to kill your dream. And often your decision is made in the choices you make about where you will invest your time and energy. What are you choosing today? Choose success.

Let God Guide You to Freedom

After spending 40 years in China, Henry Poppen was called into the main city square for a public trial. Over ten thousand people jammed the streets as accusation after accusation was read against him. Finally, he was declared guilty on all counts and was told he must leave the country.

He and his wife were put on a bus and sent to Swatow. They were hoping to board a steamer and leave for freedom in Hong Kong and then head back to America. But in Swatow he was pulled off the bus, placed in solitary confinement in a little cell that measured only six feet by eight feet. The ceiling was so low, he could not stand up. He didn't know what was going to happen to him, but he did know that most missionaries who were declared the political prisoners of Mao Tse-tung never lived to tell about it.

His wife was put on a train, then a boat and finally found herself in Hong Kong. She waited anxiously in a hotel, not knowing where her husband was. Meanwhile, Dr. Poppen spent hour after hour and day after day in this small cell. He kept his sanity by singing and reciting, "I will lift mine eyes unto the hills, from whence cometh my help. My help cometh from the Lord, which made heaven and earth" (Psalms 121:1, 2).

Finally, he could stand the blackness and the mental torture no longer. At midnight he got on his hands and knees by his small, wooden cot and prayed, "Oh, God, you know I am not St. Paul, or the Apostle John or St. Peter. I am only Henry Poppen, and Henry Poppen can take no more. Lord, deliver me or take my life."

He fell asleep on his hands and knees only to be awakened about an hour later by the squeaking hinges on the door of his cell. The guards came in and tied a rope around his neck with a slipknot, ran it down his backbone and bound his arms behind him so tightly that if he struggled at all he would strangle himself. Then they led him down a dark, winding, cobblestone street. He was certain he was headed for his execution until he saw the reflection of light in the rippling water and heard the hum and chunking of an engine. Then he saw the dark outline of an ocean steamer, waiting with its gangplank down. The guards shoved him onto the deck and said, "Now get out of our country!"

The gangplank was raised and the steamer blew the whistle. The captain took the rope off his neck and cut it loose from his hands. Then he directed Poppen to his private quarters and told him to stay there. When the captain returned for him, Henry asked, "Where are we?" Through the open door, he could see the dawn breaking over the city of Hong Kong.

The captain told him that as soon as the ship was tied up at the dock, he was to run down the crowded streets and get lost. His heart jumped with joy as he realized he was free! God had heard his cry and given him *the gift of the open door!*

What greater gift can God give to anyone than the gift of the open door? God looks at your past, at your weaknesses and failures and He offers you an open door to freedom. Where you have tried and failed in the past, you can believe God today! By faith, walk through the open door, for with God all things are possible.

Good Time to Meet Him

"As a wing commander in Southeast Asia, I rose to a real crest of power and glory!" explained Colonel Bottomly. "One day I was so proud that I felt I could violate the rules of war. In spite of the president's orders, I bombed across the border in North Vietnam.

"I was called on the carpet and faced a court martial for violating the discipline of the air, which every pilot knows he cannot do," he continued. "In this terrible situation, with my whole career threatened, I remembered my son and the many times that he had tried to tell me about God's love.

"So I called my son long distance and asked him to tell me more about this loving and forgiving God. And since then my life has changed! Miracles started to happen! My whole outlook on life has changed!"

Near tragedy finally forced this colonel to look at the really big issues in life. He discovered a loving God. How about you? Have you stopped long enough to meet God? Today's a good time to do so.

Plan Your Future

A young boy approached a wealthy contractor standing on the sidewalk surveying the tall office structure he was building. "Tell me, sir," the lad said, "how can I be successful like you when I grow up?"

The gray-haired builder smiled kindly, then answered, "Easy, son. Buy a red shirt and work like crazy!" Knowing the youngster didn't understand, the wealthy builder of skyscrapers pointed to the skeleton of his rising new structure. "See all those men up there? See that man in the red shirt? I don't even know his name. But I've been noticing how hard he works. One of these days I'm going to need a new superintendent, and I'll go to that fellow and say, 'Hey, you in the red shirt, come here!' He'll get the opportunity!"

Most people fail, not because they lack talent, money or opportunity, they fail because they never really planned to succeed. Plan your future, even if it means wearing a red shirt! You are the one who has to live there!

Don't Wait Too Long

An old story tells about a flock of geese heading south to escape the coming winter. The first night they landed in a farmer's yard and filled themselves with corn. When morning came, they flew on—all except one.

This goose said, "The corn is so good. I will stay one more day, for there may not be much corn up ahead." He stuffed himself that day, and the next morning, he decided to wait still another day. This went on until he had developed the habit of saying, "Tomorrow I will fly south."

Then came the inevitable day when the winds of winter became so severe that waiting any longer would mean certain death for the goose. He stretched his wings, waddled across the barnyard and attempted to pick up enough speed to fly. But alas! He was too fat to fly! He had waited too long!

Today is the day you should begin! Decide now to be a success. Set your mind free from locked-in thinking.

Tackle Those Problems

You didn't ask to be born! You had nothing to do with your parentage, the color of your skin, your national origin, your station in life and probably not even with where you are living. But God has been guiding you. He has a plan for you.

Dare to believe that! Trust God confidently. You can be a saint in Caesar's household. You can bloom where you are planted. God will use you if you trust him. So throw away your wastebasket and replace it with a tackle box. Tackle your problems positively, creatively and prayerfully!

God wants every flower to bloom. He wants every seed to sprout. He wants every person to be happy.

Frozen on Life's Highway

Mrs. Schuller and I were in Europe for a special conference. After the meeting, we flew to Milan, Italy, where we rented a car to go to Padua. We wanted to see the organ that was being built for our church. The pipe organ had been under construction for a couple of years. It was recently installed and is a marvellous instrument.

We landed in Milan, picked up our rental car and drove onto the highway which is only a half mile from the airport. We started sailing down this eight-lane road because we were late for our appointment in Padua.

Suddenly the traffic started slowing down, and we could see across the highway—tollgates. We didn't expect a toll road! Now we were only about 150 feet from the tollgates. I suddenly remembered we had neglected to do something any international traveler knows must be done. We had neglected to cash a traveler's check into Italian money. All we had was some Swiss money and some American dollars.

I asked my wife, "Do you think they'll take Swiss money or American dollars?" She laughingly said, "You know they won't." "How about traveler's checks?" And she shook her head and laughed again.

Well, as it happened, they would only take Italian money. But God had a solution to our problem. While we were waiting in the traffic for the cars to go through, we stopped the engine. When the car ahead of us drove on, we started the motor and put the car in gear, only to find that we couldn't move. Mrs. Schuller, who was driving, said, "The car won't move." "Is it on?" I asked. "Have you got it in first gear?" She revved up the motor and said, "Yes." The car jolted, but the wheels wouldn't move. "Try reverse," I suggested. She put it in reverse and we still didn't move.

"Relax, dear," I told her. "We'll play it cool and calm.

We don't speak Italian. Any minute now somebody is going to come out and offer us help."

Without exaggeration, we waited more than 60 minutes. People drove all around us and shouted all kinds of things. Finally, a wrecking truck appeared down the road and came to our rescue. He pulled us four miles off to a repair place. By the time we got there, smoke was coming from the back wheels. All four brakes were frozen. I was grateful we had broken down where we could be seen, rather than later, on some desolate stretch of highway.

There are many people who are stuck like that right now on the highway of life. Perhaps you feel that you are not moving ahead. You're frozen where you are. Traffic is passing you by. Only God is capable of coming to your rescue and unlocking your wheels. When you place your life in His hands and trust Him, you will discover that every problem is an opportunity—an opportunity to move ahead to some new adventure or new relationship. Believe God today. He'll get you moving again!

Eager to Meet People

People often ask me if I ever have problems meeting people or making new friends and acquaintances. My immediate response is: "No, because God has given me a powerful imagination!"

I discovered this technique in starting our church. With only Mrs. Schuller and I as members, I decided to go down the street and ring doorbells, telling my story to people face-to-face. At first I trembled at the thought of going from door to door, speaking with strangers. Then God sparked my imagination!

I began to visualize wonderful people on the other side of the doors—people who were eager to meet a new minister. And that did it!

Try this technique with a problem person. Imagine this potential enemy as a fine person at heart. And that's exactly what he'll become!

Don't Listen to Losers

Some time ago I visited a school where all the students were Down's-syndrome children. The founder of this educational facility believed with a passion that these handicapped youngsters could learn some of the things that normal children enjoy doing.

I was excited as I watched these kids learning to read and write whole sentences. For weeks, my enthusiasm carried over into my conversations with friends.

But one man, who was a friend and colleague, reacted with the most bitter, angry and negative statements. I was stunned by his bleak response. Later, I learned that he had a Down's-syndrome child, and he and his wife were advised to institutionalize him. "He's hopeless," they were told.

Then I could understand his grief. He had listened to negative thinking, hopeless advice. And when he heard that there were some people who offered hope and believed in the possibilities of these special children, their success passed judgment on what he had done.

Don't listen to the losers! Get in touch with people who are positive and filled with *hope!*

Enthusiasm Is God's Gift

Enthusiasm is that mysterious something that turns an average person into an outstanding individual. Enthusiasm lifts us from fatigue to energy, pulls us from mediocrity to excellence, turns a bright light on our lives until our faces glow and our eyes sparkle. It's a spiritual magnet that draws happy people to us and a joyful fountain that bubbles and causes people to come to our sides and share our joy.

Out of this fountain there leaps a self-confidence that shouts to the world, "I can! It's possible! Let's go!" Enthusiasm is the long-sought-after fountain of youth. Old men who stop to drink of its elixir suddenly dream new dreams, and mysterious energy surges through the body that moments before was fatigued, weary and old. It's a source of energy that never runs out.

Drink from this fountain of enthusiasm, and you will experience a miracle. Discouragement will fade away like the morning's fog in the noonday sun. Suddenly you start laughing, whistling and singing. You know you are a child of God.

Enthusiasm—when someone offers it to you, take it, especially if you don't want it. Enthusiasm is God's beautiful gift to you!

Listen to Your Emotions

As the artist finished the final detail in his winter scene, he stepped back to admire his work. It was magnificent! Every detail fit perfectly—the trees were heavy under the coating of snow and ice, icicles gracefully draped the edges of the cabin roof, and carefully balancing the composition were drifts of freshly blown snow in the foreground.

But the painting hung in the gallery for months. No one bought it, even though the artist's reputation was based primarily on his winter scenes.

"What's wrong with it?" he asked another artist who stood looking at the picture. "Give me a brush," his friend replied. She took the brush and mixed some colors, and then with a skillful dab, she added a touch of red to the window of the cabin. Then some grey paint was quickly transformed into some wisps of smoke coming out of the chimney. Within a day, the painting was sold!

What had been cold and forbidding suddenly became warm and inviting. Two touches changed the emotional tone. We are emotional creatures, and unless we are alive emotionally, we are not experiencing life. Listen to your emotions. They are a basic and essential part of you!

Seed-Thoughts of Life

Anyone can count the seeds in an apple, but only God can count the apples in one seed! There are infinite possibilities in little beginnings if God is involved.

Every human being is a potential receptacle for God's voice. Our brains are designed so that we have the capacity to think and receive God's ideas and thoughts.

When God gives you an idea, He is scattering seeds into your life. If we plant the seeds by faith, they can grow into new health, strength, abundance and prosperity. God does His biggest miracles through His smallest people. That's the miracle of the apple seed!

How many apple trees are hidden in the seed-thoughts in your life? Nurture your ideas. Pay the price and then with God's help watch your dream grow!

Relax, Release

"Relax, Dr. Schuller, just relax," my golf teacher told me. "Why, I'm relaxed," I assured him as I gripped my club fiercely, as if it were a sword.

"Feel the muscles in the back of your legs. See how tight they are?" my instructor continued. "Now feel the muscles in your feet. I daresay they are stiff too. So are the muscles in your shoulders, arms, wrists and hands—I can see the tension! Even the muscles in your face are tight!

"Doctor Schuller, you must learn to relax," he continued as he took a deep breath and exhaled. "Mentally unwind! Loosen up the muscles in your eyelids, your lips and your entire face! Okay, now your face is relaxing. Start relaxing the muscles in your shoulders—feel the soothing, balmy, unrestrained feeling flow like warm water out of a shower over every muscle in your body. Now breathe deeply and exhale slowly. Take two more deep breaths and each time exhale slowly," he said.

He sounded silly as he repeated this process, but I did what he was telling me to do. And guess what happened? It really worked! The golf club fell right out of my hands!

"I said relax, not collapse," my instructor shouted as he picked up my five iron.

Well, I never learned to play golf very well, but those lessons did make me aware of some tension within my body that I never knew existed! And only as we become sensitive to the presence of tension will we be able to begin to do something positive about these negative emotions and forces.

Here is a fundamental principle: Creativity does not occur in a tense environment. Tranquility is the mental climate that releases your ability to be creative.

Joy in the Darkness

"It's been two years now since I lost my eyesight," the lovely young girl enthused, "and do you know what I've discovered? I have found out that most unhappy thoughts come from seeing!"

Her face radiated with joy as she continued, "Before my accident I saw women wearing expensive clothes, and I became dissatisfied with what I had. I noticed beautiful people, and I was unhappy with my own appearance.

"Then it came to me," she added. "Most joy-producing thoughts come into people's minds in the dark! You close your eyes when you kiss the one you love. You close your eyes when you listen to soft music. You close your eyes when you talk to God. I don't really need to see to enjoy life!"

Try closing your eyes today. Listen to the sounds around you. Think about lovely things. Take some time and thank God for all of His goodness. Then throw back your shoulders and face life today filled with the joy that comes from the simple things in life!

Problems Into Possibilities

"Reverend, I've got so many problems! I just wish I could go someplace where there are no problems."

My minister-friend told this despondent businessman, "I know a place near here that has a population of 15,000 people, and not one person has a problem!"

"Where? I'm ready to move, just tell me where it is," the man enthused.

"Well," my friend continued, "it's the cemetery right down at the end of this street."

Problems are a part of life. And the possibility thinker knows that problems are the challenges that keep us young and spare us from lifeless boredom. A person who faces no problems in life faces no challenges. And the one who faces no challenges is also the one who experiences no excitement in life.

When you think big, set beautiful goals and then dare to try, you will also be creating problems. The size of your problems will be in direct proportion to the size of your dream. But those problems are opportunities that spell possibilities! Stay alive! Live adventurously!

Look to the Reward

A strong, vibrant American boy trained vigorously for the Munich Olympics. His dream was to return home with a gold medal in at least one of the swimming events. But one week before the games were to begin, one of his lungs collapsed while he was working out.

Following the operation, the doctors said he shouldn't even go in the water for at least two weeks. But he would not be stopped! He continued to work out, looking beyond his pain and weakness to a gold medal.

On the day of his event, the announcer called out the names for the 200-meter freestyle swim competition. His name was called—and he stepped proudly onto the starting block.

The gun went off. At the half-way mark, he was tied with the leader. But it was at that turn that he brushed the wall and ripped his stitches open. It threw off his timing, but he kept on swimming and took second place. By the time the Olympics were finished, he had a gold, silver and a bronze medal hanging around his neck!

When you look beyond to the reward, you forget about the pain!

Unlock Hidden Possibilities

A maid was hired to clean an artist's studio each night. Every evening she would come in to sweep up the chips off the floor and clean the room.

Each evening, she was fascinated by the emerging form of a person out of a chunk of marble. She saw the shape of the head, then the features of a face. Gradually, the head of a man began to take on a familiar form.

One night she came in just as the artist was ready to leave. For the first time she saw the fully sculptured form. "Why, that's Abraham Lincoln," she exclaimed. "How did you know Mr. Lincoln was in there?"

We chuckle at her reaction. But there is truth in her statement. For God looks at you and sees far more inside you than you can even imagine. Let Him unlock your hidden possibilities. Set your potential free. He is the sculptor!

Success More Than Luck

Four times a year ministers from around the world attend our Institute for Successful Church Leadership here on the campus of the Garden Grove Community Church. And one thing that really surprises me is that many of them attribute our success to "luck." That's just ridiculous!

Our successful and growing ministry didn't just happen. Together with God, we planned it this way. We have a two-year plan, a five-year plan and a ten-year plan. We think ahead! In selecting our goals we do it prayerfully. We ask God to unfold His plan and then wait for some answers.

What is occurring today is small compared to what will be happening five years from now. This ministry will be touching more lives, solving more problems, saving more souls, preventing more suicides and healing more marriages than ever before. For nothing succeeds like success!

Broken Hearts Can Be Mended

There is a lady in our church whom I affectionately call "Mom." Years ago, Mom Schug adopted me because I am the same age as her only son. He was killed in World War II when a Japanese kamikaze pilot made a suicide dive onto the deck of a United States aircraft carrier. With all of my family in Iowa, she has also been a grandmother, especially to my two youngest daughters. We all love her dearly.

One day I was reading an article about a man who was a Japanese kamikaze pilot whose turn to fly a mission never arrived. The war ended a day too early. As I read about him, I was impressed with his positive attitude. He struck me as a genuine possibility thinker, so I got in touch with him and invited him to speak at a meeting in our church.

When Mom Schug found out what I did, she became very angry with me. "That's one service I absolutely refuse to attend," she sternly informed me.

But when I stood to introduce our guest speaker, I noticed Mom sitting right in the front pew. Her gaze was fixed intently on the man as he approached the podium. I could tell she had mixed feelings about being there.

When the man finished talking to our group, he went and stood near the door, where people could greet him. He was quickly surrounded by a crowd of people with additional questions. I was certain Mom had slipped out, but was surprised to see her standing silently near the fringe of the crowd. She waited patiently for everyone to leave.

Finally, she stood before the man and started talking with him. His head went back, as if in shock or anger. But as I watched, I noticed the smile on his face. He reached out and with tears in both their eyes, they hugged each other!

The barrier was broken! The anger and hurt that Mom had harbored in her heart for years was set free. Only love can mend a broken heart, and hers was whole once again. Together, they experienced a bond of love that only God can give.

God is alive today! Allow Him to come into your life, and you will be overpowered by a love that will not let you believe anything but the best about the worst!

Make Good Things Happen

Locked-in thinkers are people who sit around waiting for success to happen, and when they don't succeed, they complain.

I'm thinking of two salesmen I know. When I drop by to see one of them, I usually find him sitting behind a desk with his legs crossed. "How's business?" I ask. "Oh, pretty good," he answers, glumly.

The other salesman is a different sort. When I ask him how business is, he says, "Great!" But he doesn't just sit behind his desk. I always find him on the telephone, working on his prospect list. He's adding names of people who could possibly need what he's selling. He discovered that the good salesmen make sales happen!

People who live in a super life make it happen! They plant seeds, make calls, write letters. They are aggressive and on the move. They don't wait for success to find them. They find success!

You Can Do It Here and Now

Have you ever wished you had somebody else's job? Or could live in another city?

When I was in New York, I talked with a young executive who enthusiastically said to me, "I'm moving to California—that's where the real opportunities are today!" I smiled and related to him what another businessman had said just two weeks earlier. We were having lunch together when he enthused, "I've almost worked out the details of my transfer to New York—that's where the power centers are. And that's where the opportunities abound!"

Look at the great movements of history. Why have so many started in remote and little-known areas? Because attitude is more important than latitude in determining how successful you will be. What you are counts more than where you are!

Beginning today, ask yourself this question every morning: "What can I do with what I have where I am?" Then let your imagination run free. There are all kinds of things you can do. And before you know it, your place will become an international headquarters for a work, a business or a movement! Bloom where you are planted!

Soar Above Obstacles

The great violinist Paganini was performing before a distinguished audience when suddenly a string on his violin snapped. The audience was startled, but the master musician, unruffled, continued to play on the three remaining strings.

Suddenly, another string broke. Still Paganini played without hesitation. Then, with a sharp crack, a third string snapped. The audience sat in silenced bewilderment. For a brief moment the artist stopped, raised his famous Stradivarius violin high in one hand and announced, "One string—and Paganini," and with furious skill and the matchless discipline of a superb craftsman finished the selection on the single string with such matchless perfection that the audience gave him a tumultuous ovation.

There will be times—as you pursue your goal—that one string after another will snap. But don't give up! Keep on, because the very power of the Eternal God will surge deep within your being. And you will, with His strength, achieve your objective.

Discontent Can Bring Joy

Are you content to live the rest of your life the way you are living right now?

If your answer is "yes, I'm content," then you have a problem. You are selling your life too cheaply!

But if your answer is "no, I'm not content to live the rest of my life the way it is today," then you have some great—even fantastic—possibilities ahead of you. You are ready for God to turn your life around. This life-renewing experience happens as you discover the power of possibility thinking.

Begin to believe that there is a more exciting life ahead of you, that there is more in store for your life than what you experience today. You will discover that there is more knowledge, more happiness, new opportunities, higher happiness, greater prosperity, and richer self-esteem waiting for you!

Success Is Who You Are

Success is not the opposite of failure. A runner may come in last, but if he beats his record time, he is a success!

Some people measure success by the amount of wealth a person has been able to accumulate. It's true—super-successful people often become wealthy people. But money alone does not measure success.

Super-successful people know the secret. Success is only measured by what you are, not by what you have. Everyone has within himself the potential for that kind of success!

No Such Thing as Luck

An ancient legend tells of an old man and a little boy who were riding together in a canal that followed a stream through a forest in a strange land. The wise old man picked a leaf out of the water and looked at its veins. Turning to the boy he asked, "Son, what do you know about these trees?"

"Nothing, sir, I have not studied that yet," the youngster replied.

"Well, son, you have missed twenty-five percent of your life," and he threw the leaf back into the water.

Soon they drifted close to shore, and the old man reached down and picked up a glistening wet rock. He rolled it over in his hand until it sparkled in the sun. "Son, look at the rock. What do you know about the earth?"

The boy answered, "I am sorry, sir, I have not studied that yet."

The old man threw the rock back into the water and said, "Son, you have missed another twenty-five percent of your life if you do not know about the soil. Now you are missing fifty percent of your life."

They drifted on, and dusk fell. The first star appeared in the sky. The wise man looked up and said, "Son, look at that star. Do you know its name? What do you know about the heavens?"

"I am sorry, sir, I have not studied that yet," the boy replied.

"Son, you do not know the trees, you do not know the soil, you do not know the sky, you are missing seventy-five percent of your life."

They drifted along silently for a while. Suddenly, the whispering sounds in the distance became the roar and rumble of rushing water ahead. The canoe was quickly caught up in a swift current that threw them into fast-moving rapids. The little boy yelled, "There is a waterfall ahead! You must jump!"

"But I can't swim!" the old man cried out.

"Well, then you have studied the wrong things, and you have lost all your life!" the boy exclaimed.

The old man had studied the wrong things in life. He had majored in the minors. His imaginations took him from one subject to another—all without rhyme or reason. You see, I interpret the man as being totally without goals. He didn't know where he was going, and he got exactly nowhere.

A lot of people live this way, and then they envy those who are "lucky" enough to be successful.

But life doesn't happen by chance. There is really no such thing as "luck." Opportunities come to those who are prepared to take the risks and are ready to jump into the water.

Don't allow life to pass you by today. Set your goals and then don't be sidetracked by what appears to be an interesting tangent.

Be at the Center

I have traveled in cities all across America, and one interesting observation I have made is that a certain percentage of people in each city believe that they live in the center of the world!

For instance, when I was in New York City people said, "We are the center of the world. After all New York is the World Capital!"

Then when I visited Chicago, people said, "We are the center of the United States; the country revolves around us."

In Kansas City, Missouri, people said, "We are the hub of the nation."

There is even a small town in Idaho on the Snake River that is convinced they are the "focal point of the Great Northwest."

Everybody wants to be at the center of something! And you can be, wherever you are and whoever you are. For it's not the place that matters, it's the person. Attitude, more than latitude, determines the future!

Don't Negate Your Dream

A possibility thinker never says no to any idea that holds some possibility for good! Before saying yes to a problem-plagued possibility, he may amend, modify, qualify or delay; but never will he cast an unqualified vote against any suggestion that has within it the seed of some possible positive good.

Just because it's impossible is no reason to vote no to a potentially great idea. Creativity starts when some possibility thinker challenges the problems in the positive idea that everyone else thinks is impossible.

You become your own tyrant when you surrender your will to the negative thoughts that you carelessly allow admittance into the sacred and unguarded areas of your mind! In that defenseless moment—in that irresponsible action—you become your own oppressor. No one else but you has the power to receive, welcome and nourish the dream-destroying, opportunity-abandoning, success-strangulating negative thoughts in your mind.

Of all the persons living on planet Earth, there is only one person who has the power to cast the deciding vote to kill your dream. That person is you! You can also cast that life-giving, hope-filled vote that says yes to your dream!

Meet the Challenge

People took their seats quickly as the committee chairman called the meeting to order.

The minutes were read, then the chairman opened discussion on a new project. After a long session of tossing ideas back and forth, one of the members came up with a creative, problem-solving, God-glorifying idea.

But before anyone had a chance to make comments on the great idea, one of the key members blurted out those terrible words, "That's impossible!" That negative comment killed the idea right there!

Impossibilities stop some people, but for other people the difficulties simply provide extra motivation. Don't be intimidated by problems! Challenge the impossibilities! It's possible!

No Fiddling Around

My daughter came home from school one day bragging about one of her girlfriends who played the violin. She went on and on describing her involvement in the high-school orchestra until I interrupted her and said, "Honey, would you like to take violin lessons?"

"I'd love to play the violin," she enthused, "but I wouldn't want to be just one of the violinists in the orchestra. I'd want to be in the first chair!"

"Well, why not?" I challenged half jokingly. "Use possibility thinking!" The next thing I knew she had signed up for violin lessons and was trying out for the high-school orchestra. She made it, but she started out in the tenth chair.

She worked harder and harder, until one day she came home from school and proudly announced that she had made first chair!

"It really works!" she cried out. "Possibility thinking really works!"

You Need Patience

I have discovered that the possibility perspective demands *big thinking!* So big that it often requires large amounts of patience. You need patience to hold on through tough times, especially during the perspective phase—a phase that all successful projects must go through.

I know how difficult this waiting time can be. I had a big dream of a dynamic church with a beautiful building and a Tower of Hope with a 24-hour live telephone counseling ministry. I dreamed of a staff of eight ministers, and 1,000 laypeople doing the teaching and counseling. But my dream was interrupted. All the possibility thinking I could muster left me trapped in a corner.

For two years God tested me to make sure he could trust me. That was easy for God to do. His biggest task was to keep me believing bigger and better and more beautifully than I had ever thought before. In the process, I discovered there are no mammoth tasks, only little minds!

Win With Self-Confidence

When theologians say that the core of sin is rebellion against God, they stop short of the mark. The deeper question is why would people rebel against a beautiful God? The answer is that every person is born with a negative self-image, which is reflected in an inherent distrust and a fear of failure in relationships. We tend to rebel, which is to say we set up a defense mechanism to protect ourselves from any possible relationship that appears to be threatening.

A newly born infant lacks any capacity to trust. In the first stage of development, the child begins to learn the experience of trust. Following the traumatic experience of birth, which is, when you think about it, a rude and shocking way to enter the world, the infant moves from nontrust to trust. Through soft stroking, bathing, feeding, holding, the new occupant learns, during this first year of life, that this noisy, alien world isn't so horrible after all.

During the second year—stage two—the initial feelings of trust become self-confidence. The infant learns to crawl and then, after a time, discovers how to stand. Now comes the thrill of the vertical dimension. Suddenly, the child feels tall.

In succeeding stages of his growth, the child is challenged to experience individually, to discover the ability to make choices, the power to make decisions, and learns, also, the rewards of achievement. As achievement piles on achievement, he discovers his selfhood. He tries, fails, tries again and finally learns. So he moves emotionally from lack of trust, to trust, to self-confidence.

But then, something tragic may happen. This infantile self-belief may be stunted and fail to blossom into its fullest flower. The deep-seated core of distrust may again threaten to assert itself, warning the growing person: "Be careful.

You may get hurt." Almost without knowing it, self-confidence begins to disappear in adolescence and adulthood. The resulting caution tends to further throttle and strangle self-confidence.

Self-confidence becomes supplanted by a fear of failure—which becomes a pattern, a habit. And with what devious results! The fear of failure, rising from a lack of self-trust, becomes a desire to fail. "If I don't try, I'll not fail." "If I just sit there on the end of the bench where the coach won't see me, I won't go up to the plate and strike out." "If I don't try to quit smoking, I won't fail in my efforts to kick the habit." You see how it works. The way to succeed is to fail even to try.

So a negative self-image becomes the major emotional disorder that entangles human beings in a web of failure-producing attitudes. We choose to fail because we don't dare succeed. As a result, we fail because we choose to fail.

Your biggest problem is yourself! You are the only person who can say, "It's impossible." What's the difference between a possibility and an impossibility? Quite simple: The difference is a person, an attitude, and two words. The person is you! The attitude is *"I can."* The two words are *"I will."* Your deepest desire is to love yourself. If you love yourself, you will believe in yourself. If you will believe in yourself, you will believe in God, and you will think it's possible!

Walk With the Giver of Hope

While I was in Calcutta some years ago, I went to visit Mother Theresa's "Home of the Dying." When Mother Theresa saw people dying in the streets of Calcutta, she dragged their dying bodies into a deserted temple which she had cleaned up, and there she loved them until they passed away. "Every human being at least deserves to have somebody loving them while they are dying," she said. I had heard her story, and I wanted to visit her.

When I arrived, the place was filled with men in one section and women in another. There were narrow, low-lying ceilings. But the rooms smelled clean and sweet. This is what the nurses told me: "Doctor Schuller, an interesting thing is happening. We only take people here who are dying, people with terminal diseases. But the amazing thing is, when they come here, they feel the love of Christ, and they get hope, and they stop dying. We're going to have to change the name of the place from the "Home of the Dying" to the "Home of the Living."

What an incredible power hope is. God is the giver of hope. Walk with Him and begin living.

God Is Your Friend

I love people who find creative solutions to problems. I read recently about a railroad express clerk near Redwood Falls, Minnesota, whose last name was Sears. One day he received a whole box of watches to be delivered to the jeweler in town. But the shipment was in error. So Sears wrote back to the Chicago distributor and asked, "What shall I do with them?" The businessman in Chicago said, "The postage is too expensive, so for a few bucks apiece you can have them."

The railroad clerk turned his problem into an opportunity. He invented a creative, redemptive solution. He simply put together a catalog, drew some pictures, sent them to all the other railroad clerks, and they bought his watches. It was so successful, he ordered more watches and enlarged his catalog. We know it today as the Sears, Roebuck catalog.

Some of you will never have the power to invent solutions and overcome the temptation to consent to or resent problems until you begin to believe that God has control of your life. He is planning in such a way that even a dark time can be turned into a beautiful scene.

I'll tell you why I'm a possibility thinker—I know that God is my friend.

See Opportunity

David is a good friend of mine. He used to be a normal, active high schooler before he was stricken with a serious disease. As a result, his lifestyle changed rapidly. He lost most of his eyesight and was confined to a wheelchair.

But David did not let this get him down. He turned his problems into opportunities! He stayed in school and aimed for graduation. Classmates carried him and his wheelchair up and down the stairs to his classes. Friends took turns reading assignments out loud so he could pass his exams.

When graduation day finally arrived, the entire student body jumped to their feet and applauded as the principal awarded David his high-school diploma.

Anybody can be an instrument in God's hands if they choose to be! Positive thinking people expect problems but they see them as opportunities instead of obstacles!

You Need Not Gamble

A depressed and discouraged man in seedy-looking clothing was sitting on the corner of a busy street, glaring at a torn piece of newspaper. People from all walks of life hurried up and down the sidewalk, ignoring him.

Suddenly a young girl stopped, bent down, whispered, "Chin Up!" into his ear and slipped two dollars into his hand. Before he could even raise his head to thank her, she was gone. The next day she passed the same corner and tried to hurry on past the old man who was sitting in the same spot. He recognized her immediately and cried out, "Hey, Lady!" She kept on walking as if she didn't hear him. "Hey, Lady!" he bellowed out again, as she stopped and turned around. He ran toward her, waving something in the air. Out of breath, he smiled and handed her a ten-dollar bill.

"Lady," he excitedly said, "you were right!" It was Chin Up in the third race!"

To that old man, all of life was a gamble. A long shot where you ultimately lose. But you have a choice: You don't have to gamble on life. The person whose life is centered on God knows there is more—much more. "If you do this you will experience God's peace, which is far more wonderful than the human mind can understand" (Philippians 4:7 LB).

You Can Choose
to Think Big

Several years ago we bought a new home. We were so excited! We moved in as quickly as we could, and for a while only our house and the one next door were occupied. All the other homes in the tract were vacant.

Being raised on a farm, my first task was to landscape the barren ground. There was a parkway between the curb and the sidewalk that was 12 feet wide and 80 feet across. For several weeks, we discussed what we could do with that area. Finally, Mrs. Schuller suggested, "Let's pave it with bricks. We'll never have to feed it, or weed it, or mow it. And the bricks will add some charm to the front." She quickly convinced me.

Now possibility thinking says that first you make the right decisions. Then you solve the problems. So once we made the decision, it was then up to me to solve the problems.

One of the first things I found out was that you can't just lay the bricks on the ground. If you did that, the bricks would sink into the earth several inches with the first good rainstorm. I was told that before I could put the bricks down, I would have to excavate 10 inches of dirt, fill the area with eight inches of sand, and then place the bricks over the sand.

Well, that made the job a little less desirable. But we had made our decision. And the more I put off getting started, the more my wife started preaching my own sermons to me. "Beginning is half-done," she said. "Inch by inch, anything's a cinch," she continued. Finally, I got up one Monday morning, determined to begin.

I got the wheelbarrow and a shovel and approached my

task from one corner of the parkway. I had a couple of shovelfuls of dirt in the wheelbarrow when my neighbor pulled out of his driveway, came up alongside the curb and asked, "Are you going to plant a tree?" "No," I answered and then described my plan.

That's when he hit me with future shock. "What are you going to do with all that dirt?" he asked. I played it cool on the outside, but my mind was churning away trying to solve my new problem. Finally I answered him. "I'm going to make a mound. Yes, I'm going to make some mounds in the back—big mounds! I like big mounds."

"Well, it'll sure be a big mound, Schuller, but the way you're doing it you'll be at it for a month of Mondays." "Not me," I shouted to him as he started to drive off, "I'm a possibility thinker!"

I shoveled two more loads of dirt into the wheelbarrow and suddenly discovered one of the great, unpublished laws of physics. And that is, when you take a previously undisturbed piece of ground and shovel it into a wheelbarrow, it multiplies 10 times. I had a hole in the ground no more than one foot square and 10 inches deep, but the wheelbarrow was overflowing with dirt. But I enthusiastically wheeled it into the backyard and dumped it.

But as I came back out front and looked at the parkway, I said, "Lord, there's got to be an easier way." And what happened next you would not believe.

Down the street came a truck, and on the door of the truck it said in big red letters: EXCAVATING AND DIRT HAULING. The driver was my center-aisle, Sunday-morning church usher. He stopped and looked at me in my grubby clothes and said, "Reverend, what happened? What are you doing here?" "Hi, Roy, this is where we moved to," I said. "What are you doing here?" And he answered, "I'm lost."

"What are you doing with the wheelbarrow?" he asked. After I told him, he suggested, "You know, that's a tough way to do it. I've got a tractor here on the truck, and I've got a skiploader in front of it. I can have that dirt out for you in no time."

"No, Roy. I know that's expensive equipment to rent, and I just don't have that kind of money." He bent down, picked up a piece of dirt that had fallen out of my over-loaded wheelbarrow and enthused, "This is good, black dirt." "Yes," I agreed. "This was an orange orchard before they built these homes, and you know how they fertilized those orchards."

"I'll tell you what I'll do, Reverend. This is good topsoil. I can sell it. I'll take it all out and haul it away for you free—in exchange for the dirt!"

If I should live to be a hundred, I shall never forget the beautiful sound of that tractor and skiploader. By 11 o'clock in the morning he had finished the job. My parkway was ready for the sand and the bricks, and his truck was over-loaded with good, rich dirt.

I was out front sweeping off the curb and whistling away when my neighbor came home for lunch. You should have seen his face! He was an instant convert to possibility thinking!

You have a choice. You can either live a life that is filled with the fun that comes by looking for possibilities or a life filled with the fear of impossibilities. But remember, an impossibility is nothing more than a big idea that hits a mind that has to think bigger! So think big! Possibility thinking really works!

Index